# FIRING BACK

**TAKING ON** THE **PARTY BOSSES** AND **MEDIA ELITE**
TO **PROTECT OUR FAITH** AND **FREEDOM**

# TODD AKIN

# FIRING BACK

Published by WND Books®, Washington, D.C. WND Books is a registered trademark of WorldNetDaily.com, Inc. ("WND")

Unless otherwise indicated, scripture quotations are taken from the Holy Bible, King James Version (public domain).

Scripture quotations marked NIV are taken from the Holy Bible, New International Version®, NIV®. Copyright © 1973, 1978, 1984, 2011 by Biblica, Inc.™ Used by permission of Zondervan. All rights reserved worldwide. www.zondervan.com

Jacket design by Mark Karis. Cover photograph by Jason Winkeler.

WND Books are distributed to the trade by:
Midpoint Trade Books
27 West 20th Street, Suite 1102
New York, New York 10011
WND Books are available at special discounts for bulk purchases. WND Books, Inc., also publishes books in electronic formats. For more information call (541) 474-1776 or visit www.wndbooks.com.

First Edition
Hardcover ISBN: 978-1-936488-20-9
eBook ISBN: 978-1-936488-21-6

Library of Congress Cataloging-in-Publication Data
Akin, Todd, 1947-
Firing back : Taking on the party bosses and media elite to protect our faith and freedom / by Todd Akin.
pages cm
Includes bibliographical references and index.
ISBN 978-1-936488-20-9 (hardcover) -- ISBN 978-1-936488-21-6 (e-book)
1. Republican Party (U.S. : 1854- ) 2. Conservatism--United States. 3. Political culture--United States. 4. Religion and politics--United States. 5. United States--Politics and government.
I. Title.
JK2356.A39 2014
324.9778'044--dc23
2014012370

Printed in the United States of America
14 15 16 17 18 19  MV  9 8 7 6 5 4 3 2 1

*This book is dedicated to my parents*

## PAUL & NANCY AKIN

*Paul and Nancy Akin are outstanding examples of "The Greatest Generation."*
*They love God, family, country.*

*During WW II, Paul left Harvard to serve under General Patton. On leave,*
*he met and married Nancy Bigelow. After the War, choosing duty over his*
*love of sailing and the sea, they moved to the St. Louis area for him to serve*
*in a leadership position at Laclede Steel. There, they raised four boys. Dad*
*retired as CEO, earned an M.Div., and became a pastor. Mum, devoted*
*wife and mother, is known for her gracious hospitality, Bible studies, love*
*of nature and beautiful gardens.*

*Together, they taught their boys to: "see what needs to be done and do it,"*
*work hard and not be dependent on others, courageously resist bad peer*
*pressure, put duty over personal preference, and above all else, be honest.*

*Long-time Patriots and Believers saved by grace, Paul and Nancy Akin are*
*handing a bright torch to their thirteen great grandchildren.*

# CONTENTS

# FOREWORD

**F**iring Back is aptly named for a book by my friend Todd Akin. Todd didn't ask for a war with the party establishment, but he sure did get one. No one in American politics knows better than I do the immediate bias and attacks that come from liberals and the media establishment when Christians with sincere convictions make a move into the political arena. We've learned to deal with their attacks and have even come to expect them. More shocking are the attacks on social conservatives from party bosses, partisan power brokers and the entrenched GOP establishment. I'm deeply offended by this infighting within the Republican Party, because it is destructive to the country we care so deeply about.

Todd Akin served as a strong and brave voice for conservative causes during his twelve years in the US House. But when he ran for the US Senate, the establishment wasn't happy because they hadn't picked him. Too often establishment players want the support and votes of social conservatives—we can sit on the bus (in the back!), but they don't want us to drive the bus! Todd wasn't the first pick of party gurus to take on Claire McCaskill in Missouri and consequently was considered a long shot. He campaigned on his values and carried an unapologetically patriotic message of hope for America. Unlike many candidates, Todd never said anything negative about his Republican opponents, and although he was outspent four to one, he won his primary handily.

Unfortunately, it wasn't long before his wrong choice of words in a live TV interview on the sensitive topic of rape became an opportunity for his opponents to seize his mistake and try to use it to force him out of the race. Don't get me wrong. I think it would have been better if Todd hadn't gone in that direction in answering the question he was asked. However, having been in the public spotlight and simply as a human I know what it is to say the wrong thing. I've wanted a "do over" more than once on how I answered a question, and I've been the target of others taking one statement and twisting it to imply I must believe something or using it to narrowly define me in a terrible way. I expected Democrats to pounce on Todd. But I was disheartened and outraged when Republicans circled the wagon—not to support Todd and help him overcome an obstacle but instead as a firing squad pointed at the congressman.

Many in the Republican establishment still bruised that they didn't beat Todd in the primary, saw this as their opportunity to take him out and select someone more palatable to their tastes. There is something terribly ironic when the winning candidate in a primary who refused to say anything negative about his Republican opponents is attacked by one prominent Republican after another. They sharpened their knives and got in line to repeatedly stab him in the back. Now, after the race, they are still saying, "See, conservatives can't get elected!" This infuriates me. In order to move America forward, we have to remember that we are on the same team, and we have to learn to agree most of the time about most of the things we hold dear.

What I admire most about Todd is the kind of man he is and his courageous battle for his convictions. Todd and his wife Lulli are sincere in their faith and their love for our country. Todd entered politics for all the right reasons and during his time of service he never sold out to special interest. He never longed to fit in or become a part of the Washington club. He stayed true to his God, his faith and family, and the principles he believes in. Todd didn't grow bitter or desperate. His character never wavered during what proved to be very trying days of his campaign. I can't adequately express how admirable and refreshing that is to me. Todd represented to me what we must do more of as conservatives. We must stand up for what we believe in. We must no longer apologize for our principles or skate around them in fear of protest. There is a quiet majority out there in need of voices—they are looking for men and women willing to stand for what is right and to offer our nation the leadership it most desperately needs.

Todd's campaign is also a lesson to us as why, as conservatives, we must not tolerate back-room politics, party bosses and establishment elitism running the show. Too much is at stake to reduce our efforts to partisan power struggles and party politics. Our nation is rich with the history of sacrifice. Our advancement and progress is the result of great generations before us choosing principle over convenience, right over wrong and good over evil. Our nation's future is at stake and the days we live in require that we too fight the good fight, sacrifice, offer ourselves, endure difficulty and when necessary, Fire Back.

—*Governor Mike Huckabee, 2014*

# INTRODUCTION

n my campaign for the US Senate in 2012, incredible as it seems in retrospect, I spoke a few words that touched off an explosion heard around the world. As the dust settled, the mainstream media ridiculed me, the leadership of the Republican Party denounced me, and many true patriots defended me.

In this book I share the inside story of that political assassination. I have attempted to provide context, share some pointed anecdotes, and explain the highs and lows of politics from the perspective of a longtime patriot and twelve-year US congressman.

Though we lost the general election, conservatives should not be discouraged. I held public office for twenty-four years as an unapologetic conservative. Other patriots can do likewise.

The events described in this story are unusual because of the magnitude of media reaction, the thoroughness of the Republican attacks in a general election, and the courage of many patriotic Americans who stood with me. But more than that, these events serve as an opportunity for those who love America to reconsider our responsibilities as citizens, confront the changes that must take place, and chart a course for a bright future.

# 1

# THE SILENCE BEFORE
# THE STORM

slept well the night of August 7, 2012, after our wonderfully joyous victory party, and woke up the next morning deeply thankful and happy. I was thankful that we had won a tough primary election for the US Senate against an opponent who had the support of many party insiders and who had outspent us 4 to 1. I was thankful that we had not compromised our values about honest, positive campaigning. I was proud of my son Perry, who had taken time off from work to manage the campaign so successfully. I was proud of my daughter Abigail, who had done such a great job orchestrating the victory party and other events. I was proud of the other members of my family who helped so much, especially my wife, Lulli, for supporting me through it all. And I was very thankful for the staffers, the volunteers, the contributors, and the friends who made it such a splendid victory.

We were now squared off against the incumbent Democratic senator Claire McCaskill, and the media were determined to deny us the satisfaction that comes with victory. *Politico* headlined its story on the race, "Missouri GOP Senate Primary: McCaskill gets her opponent, Akin wins."[1] The *Washington Post* assured its readers that our win would hearten national Democrats, "who have taken the unusual step of intervening in the GOP primary to elevate the congressman, whom they viewed as the GOP's weakest potential nominee of the three major candidates."[2] The media were buying the McCaskill camp spin that her ads had ensured me the victory.

The transition from a primary campaign to the general was harder than I thought. It was like switching from two skis to one when you are waterskiing. There is that moment when your balance is precarious, and your confidence is as shaky as your balance. What made the transition shakier still was that the Missouri GOP and the Senate Republican Campaign Committee sent their own people to the campaign to help out. As well intentioned as they were, these outsiders inevitably caused some friction with the existing staff. I trusted Perry to mesh this new team together, but I also knew he was up to his eyeballs in campaign details already.

As our campaign team transitioned to the general election, our focus was now on beating Claire McCaskill. Our task was aided by her support for Obamacare. In 2008 John McCain carried Missouri, and the state was getting redder by the year. Obamacare was very unpopular, and this issue was helping to shift the state away from liberalism. In a 2010 referendum, by a three-to-one margin, Missouri voters rejected the mandatory health insurance part of the administration's health care plan. Nevertheless, McCaskill still publically supported that plan. She was one of the first to support Obamacare in the state and did so quite publically. Now her name was associated with Obamacare and the baggage that went with it. The national Democrats thought she was vulnerable. So did the national Republicans. On the ground in Missouri, we knew her position on Obamacare would be a vulnerability, but it would still be a fight.

Despite McCaskill's position on Obamacare, she had some strengths. She had a strong statewide organization and plenty of name identification among the voters. In 2006 she had beaten incumbent Jim Talent. Then as now, her campaign coffers were flowing over with money. In this race she didn't have to spend money to beat a primary opponent because she hadn't had one. She just stockpiled her money, of which she had received a lot from across the country. Some leftist groups viewed her as a feminist role model; this was especially true of women's groups whose primary mission, twisted as it sounds, was to ensure that women could continue to kill their unborn babies with impunity. These groups liked McCaskill and sent her money. To beat her, we would need a good team, and we would need a lot of money. The Republican leaders had money and promised to help us out.

What I didn't realize was just how quickly these promises for support could disappear. Many Republican leaders in the establishment don't like political candidates who stand on principle. A principled politician might not agree to their various backroom deals. Sharron Angle from Nevada had learned this lesson. During the campaign I had a chance to meet with her, and we talked about her run for the US Senate in Nevada in 2010. Her race in some ways anticipated what I would experience in 2012.

In June 2010, Angle won the Nevada Republican primary and, with it, the right to face Senate Majority Leader Harry Reid in the November general election. The day after her primary win, Angle was leading Reid by eleven points in the polls. Yet, as a strong pro-life conservative who was endorsed by the Club for Growth, Angle proved much too outspoken for those timid souls who believe Republicans should just go along and get along. Even before her primary victory, Sig Rogich, a former high-level staffer for both Ronald Reagan and George H. W. Bush, started a "Republicans for Reid" organization. "I could never support somebody who espouses the radical positions that Angle does," said Rogich, but apparently he could support a senator who, even the Associated Press acknowledged, was "a highly visible symbol of what many Nevadans consider to be a liberal, big-spending Obama agenda."[3]

The Republican mayors of Sparks and Reno signed on to Rogich's subversive cause, as did many other Republican dignitaries, and Angle's numbers started to tumble. With Republicans denouncing Angle, Reid could just sit back and enjoy the show. As

Angle told me, the national party promised a lot more than it delivered. She believed, and this I cannot confirm, that Senate minority leader Mitch McConnell made a deal with Reid to undercut Angle's run for office. When Reid finally beat Angle 50 to 45 percent, those Republicans for Reid took the outcome as a sign that Angle was too conservative for Nevada. No, she was too principled for opportunists like them. Angle's courage and conviction would have made her an excellent senator.

My schedule ramped up quickly, and I had little time to ponder the past Senate race from Nevada. On the first weekend after the election, I joined a barnstorming bus tour with all of Missouri's statewide candidates, and we hit all the hot spots. In St. Charles, Missouri senator Roy Blunt joined us. He told the crowd what a great guy I was and how, when we were both in the House, we used to compete to be Missouri's most conservative congressman. According to Blunt, sometimes I won as most conservative; sometimes he did. This neck-and-neck race was news to me, to my staff, and probably to his staff too.

A week later I found myself on another group tour, this one organized by Rep. Billy Long, a Republican from southwest Missouri. Among the stops was the traditional Governor's Ham Breakfast at the Missouri State Fair. Although no candidate was permitted to speak at the event, nearly a thousand Missourians showed up, which made it a prime meet-and-greet event. At the event, reporters questioned me on my opposition to the Farm Bill, particularly the part of the bill that had nothing to do with farms but covered school-lunch and food-stamp programs. On the question of school lunches, I gave the answer any prudent conservative should give. "Why not do it at the state level?" I asked. "The federal government should be out of the education business."

I have misgivings about the school-lunch program in general. There is no doubt it diminishes the role of the parent, but I bit my tongue on that. Not surprisingly, the *St. Louis Post-Dispatch* headlined its story on the breakfast, "Akin says federal government shouldn't pay for school lunches." The reporters then ran to McCaskill, who responded with the profound comment, "I think school lunches are a part of the education system."[4] For good measure, the newspaper threw in an editorial and promoted it on the front page with the scare-inducing headline, "Akin tries to turn back the clock on child hunger."[5]

In a sense, the editors were right. I would like to turn the clock back to the days when parents were responsible enough to feed their own children. Most still are. Instead of dealing with those who aren't, we have increased the dependency of millions of potentially self-supporting families, billed the taxpayers, and footed future generations with the debt for food that should be provided at home or, if not at home, then by local or state agencies.

My position was just common sense, and it was clearly consistent with the principles of federalism. Roy Blunt, who was allegedly "as conservative as Akin" a week earlier in St. Charles, took me to the woodshed. He said if I made another "gaffe" like that, the state party would not support me. He was all business.

No, Roy, a "gaffe" is when you say, as President Obama once did, "It is just wonderful to be back in Oregon. And over the last fifteen months we've traveled to every corner of the United States. I've now been in fifty-seven states? I think one left to go."[6] Or a "gaffe" is when you say, as then senator Joe Biden did, "In Delaware, the largest growth of population is Indian Americans moving from India. . . . You cannot go to a 7-Eleven or a Dunkin' Donuts unless you have a slight Indian accent. I'm not joking."[7] Or a "gaffe" is when you say, as Harry Reid once did, that Obama could be successful because he was "light skinned" and spoke "with no Negro dialect, unless he wanted to have one."[8]

Were Obama a Republican, the media would have hung his "fifty-seven states" comment around his neck as quickly as you could say "potatoe."[9] Were Biden a Republican, his observation on the work habits of Indian Americans would have cost him his career. Were Reid a Republican, we would not have heard a word about

Sharron Angle's "gaffes," but only about his.

What I said was not a gaffe at all, but a clear statement of conservative principle. Often, the very same pundits who criticize the lack of clarity and substance in political campaigns are the first ones to attack people like me who have tried to add both. And as I was just about to learn for myself, the Republicans are sometimes quicker to the attack than even the Democrats.

# 2

# DEFCON 1

lthough its events would change my life, Sunday, August 19 started innocently enough. Lulli and I got up, had breakfast, and went to services at Twin Oaks Presbyterian Church in St. Louis County. After church we came home and had lunch. After lunch I took a nap, slept soundly, and woke up happy. It was great to be home, great to be able to catch up with family. Sunday is special at our house. It is a day for worship and for rest, and on this steamy August day, after a hard-fought win in a bruising Republican senatorial primary, I needed as much rest as I could get.

As a rule, I don't watch much TV, and this Sunday I didn't watch any at all. I was fully out of the loop. My son and campaign manager, Perry, was not. Nor was my acting communications director and jack-of-all-trades, Ryan Hite. They had been monitoring the media all day. Perry had experienced a rumble or two during my twelve-year tenure in the US House of Representatives, but what he and Ryan were sensing now was a political New Madrid, an 11 on the 10-point political Richter scale.

Ryan called me later that day. His message hit me like an icy bucket of water. He said simply, "DEFCON 1" (military parlance for the highest threat level). He brought me up to speed in a few minutes, and I understood what had thrown our campaign into a war footing. Since then, I still have a hard time processing how quickly something so innocent could turn so ugly.

It was a mistake to agree to appear on Charles Jaco's Sunday morning show on Fox 2, KTVI, a St. Louis–area TV station. A veteran reporter and hard-bitten liberal, Jaco often found himself at loggerheads with local conservative activists. But since he had always treated me respectfully in the past, I considered his request. When I finally agreed, it was in large part because he was so persistent. I was well aware that the interview could be a high-risk venture, but we had just beaten two serious establishment candidates in the primary, and I was not one to shy from a healthy debate.

On Friday afternoon, August 17, 2012, I headed in to the station's suburban studio to tape the show, a little wary but not overly worried. From the first question, I could see what Jaco was trying to do, namely trap me into a sound bite that his political allies could exploit. Everyone knew this Senate race was going to be a fight, and Jaco was trying to do his part to help the liberals. Jaco raised the issue of school lunches.[1] I had opposed the Farm Bill because it was 20 percent farm and 80 percent entitlements. For this reason, as the earlier examples showed, some in the media hoped to paint me as a heartless Scrooge. On the show I questioned whether the federal government was the right entity to administer this program, the states being more efficient. I wasn't feeling as sharp as I might have been because I had just returned from a mini-vacation that my staff insisted I take. Nevertheless, I refused to give Jaco the rope with which he was hoping to hang me.

On the question of student loans, I had to correct Jaco's information. The problem wasn't that the federal government was guaranteeing the loans, but rather that it had taken over the whole program. We had seen the financial disaster of 2008 caused by government mismanagement of home loans in Fannie Mae and Freddie Mac. Why then trust the Feds to take over the student loans? We were begging for another "bubble-and-crash" scenario.

Jaco tried again with the next question on the 1965 Voting Rights Act. For the record, sixteen Democratic senators voted against the bill, but only two Republicans did. In fact, Senate Republicans cosponsored the bill. Indifferent to history, like many liberals, Jaco tried to make the case that Republicans like me opposed the Voting Rights Act. This was wrong. I did not at all agree that the act should be repealed.

"We need to make sure that every living American has the right to vote *once*," I told him in conclusion. If anything, I wanted the Voting Rights Act improved—no more dead Democratic voters, no more noncitizens, no more multiple-ballot voters. From the Voting Rights Act, Jaco moved to the Seventeenth Amendment, the one that allowed for the direct election of US senators by voters instead of by states. Once more, I stuck to my guns and avoided the killer sound bite, not that there is much public interest in that amendment in the first place. Jaco then moved on to the issue of abortion. He confirmed I was pro-life and then asked if there were any circumstance where abortion should be legal.

As an aside, abortion is very politically controversial, but it is logically very simple. Its justification rests on the answers to two questions. First, is it ever right to intentionally take the life of an innocent human being? I believe the answer is no. Most civilizations have laws against the intentional taking of life. In the Western world, those laws come from the biblical injunction "Thou shalt not kill" (Exodus 20:13). History has not been kind to those like Mao Zedong, Stalin, and Hitler, who ignored this convention.

The second question regarding abortion is, is the unborn child a "person"? The answer to this question is yes. I can speak with authority: my wife has had six Caesarean sections, and each time we found an eager young "person" inside.

I told Charles that abortion is appropriate in the case of a tubal pregnancy. The child has *no* chance of survival, I explained, but removing the child saves the mother's life. Note that the purpose of this operation is to save the mother's life. The intention is not to kill the child—that is an unavoidable consequence.

Jaco followed with the next logical question, intended to force me to take a politically unpopular position. "What about in the case of rape? Should it be legal or not?"

These are the words that triggered the cataclysmic social explosion:

> **AKIN:** If it's a legitimate rape, the female body has ways to try to shut that whole thing down. But let's assume that maybe that didn't work or something. You know, I think there should be some punishment, but the punishment ought to be on the rapist and not attacking the child.

Taking my comments in order: When a woman claims to have been raped, the police determine if the evidence supports the legal definition of "rape." Is it a legitimate claim of rape or an excuse to avoid an unwanted pregnancy? Are the police warranted to take action against a crime or not? In short, the word "legitimate" modifies the claim and not the action. There have been women who have lied about being raped, as Norma McCorvey did before the US Supreme Court. The infamous *Roe v. Wade* decision of 1972 was based on a lie.

My comment about a woman's body shutting the pregnancy down was directed to the impact of stress on fertilization. This is something fertility doctors debate and discuss. Doubt me? Google "stress and infertility," and you will find a library of research on the subject. The research is not conclusive, but there is considerable evidence that stress makes conception more difficult. And what could be more stressful than a rape?

Assuming there was pregnancy, "the punishment ought to be on the rapist": here I acknowledged that a woman can get pregnant from rape. This might surprise you, because the media lied, saying I had denied the very possibility of pregnancy from forcible rape. In fact, several fantastic young Americans who campaigned with us were themselves the products of rape. And they were thankful I would stand with them.

Lastly, the US Supreme Court ruled that the death penalty for rapists was cruel and unusual punishment.[2] The US Supreme Court prohibited capital punishment for rape in the 1977 case *Coker v. Georgia*. If it is cruel and unusual to kill the perpetrator of a violent crime, it would be many times worse to kill an innocent child.

Now, given how stupid and insulting you have been told my answer was, you would think Jaco would have jumped out of his chair and denounced me to the world. This should have been a journalistic "coup." It would have gone viral more quickly than "Bat kid saves Gotham." But here is what he said next and without so much as a raised eyebrow.

**JACO:** Let's go to the economy . . .

Jaco caught a ton of heat from his own side for not challenging my answer. The reason he did not follow up was obvious to us. He heard my answer in context with the various qualifiers.

The *Jaco Report* aired Sunday morning. I cannot imagine many people watched it. Some of those who did, texted Perry saying, "Great interview." And so, when Lulli and I drove to church, we did so without much to worry about, beyond, of course, a looming multimillion-dollar Senate race against a formidable incumbent, her ruthless aides, and a media establishment eager to feed my liver to the crocs at the St. Louis Zoo.

What happened next, I have only learned since. During that day Ryan and Perry tried to keep abreast of developments, but even they could not keep up. Apparently, KTVI-TV posted the video online that morning. A short time later, American Bridge 21st Century, a liberal political action committee, took a clip from the video and put it on YouTube. It seems someone from that PAC informed *Talking Points Memo* (TPM), which posted quotes and screen captures from American Bridge shortly after that.[3]

As a quick side note, TPM is one of those numerous, well-funded, left-leaning blogs—*Media Matters*, *Daily Kos*, and *Politico*, to name a few others—whose purpose is to feed information to their mainstream media allies that advances their shared ideological agenda. One of their chief tools is mockery. So when Sarah Palin admitted to not reading the *New York Times*, when Mitt Romney talked of the 47 percent who would not vote for him, and when then senator George Allen called a pesky tracker "Macaca," the TPMs of the world feigned outrage and spread the word. (Ironically, the American Bridge 21st Century was also the one to select the "Macaca" comment to assassinate Senator George Allen.)

Ryan got a text while he was at church from the *St. Louis Post-Dispatch*, which apparently picked up the story from TPM, asking for a comment. Within thirty minutes, "Todd Akin" was trending on Twitter. The website *Gawker* picked up the story at 2:45 p.m. Soon after, *Huffington Post* was running the video picked off the American Bridge website. Minutes after that the *Washington Post*'s political blog picked up the story. Missouri senator Roy Blunt called Perry and told him ominously, "This isn't looking good." At 4:28 p.m. Senator McCaskill officially condemned me.

"I was stunned by what he said and how he said it," claimed McCaskill. "But it opened a window into his mind and showed his beliefs. And I'm very familiar with a long list of items where Congressman Akin is outside the mainstream."[4] Outside the mainstream? Maybe in Washington, but not in Missouri. To "shorthand" my philosophy, I am an unapologetic Reagan conservative. The voters in my suburban St. Louis district understood that. I had been elected six straight times to the Missouri House and six straight times to the US House, usually with two-thirds or more of the vote.

"You know, Todd Akin would consider it an insult if you called him a moderate," McCaskill continued. "I wear the term *moderate* like a badge of honor." This was said with a straight face by a senator who voted 98 percent of the time with President Obama. Pat Buchanan later called my position on rape "the moral position of those extremists John Paul II and Ronald Reagan,"[5] but as I soon learned, it really did not matter what I had actually said in the Jaco interview, or would say in the days to come. I was the target of a media assassination, and the tactic they used comes right out of Barack Obama's communist teacher, Saul Alinsky's, playbook. "Pick the target, freeze it, personalize it, and polarize it," said Alinsky. He went on to add that "direct, personalized criticism and ridicule works."[6] The tactic is to mock, vilify, and destroy someone. The word *truth* is not mentioned once in Alinsky's twelve famed "Rules for Radicals." So it really didn't matter about what I said, or logic, or truth. I had mentioned "abortion" and "rape." That was enough. It was simply an assassination.

Thus, I was to be the point man for the fictitious "Republican war on women," because I had spoken a few words on the subject of rape and abortion. Consider the incredible hypocrisy here. Two weeks later, the Democratic Party, at their national convention, would stand and cheer for Bill Clinton, who was actually accused of sexual assault on multiple occasions. They would cheer someone who had allegedly committed multiple violent acts against women, but condemn me for saying a few words? These people have no sense of truth or justice or even common sense.

I had little time to ponder this hypocritical double standard as I began one of the most intense events of my life. What happened next in the Senate race and the decisions I made are best understood against the backdrop of my life to this point. The story begins in my early twenties, and it's quite an unusual story. Through it, you will see how my family, my faith, my past political experience, and my passion for America shaped the decisions I made and what I think should be done next.

# 3

# STIRRINGS

My classmates who knew me back at WPI, Worcester Polytechnic Institute in Massachusetts, would have been shocked to meet the Christian conservative congressman and happily married father of six children who ran for the US Senate in 2012. At WPI, when I wasn't studying engineering, which was most of the time, I was playing guitar, organizing FIJI (Phi Gamma Delta) parties, socializing, or fiddling with the Buick V6 engine I had put into my 1961 MGA. As a result, I was able to condense a four-year education into five and a half years.

Following graduation and brief service as a US Army officer, I discovered that the bad habits I had cultivated in college came at a price—act up now, pay later. By age twenty-five, I was feeling old and purposeless. It had gradually dawned on me that by living for myself I was wasting my life. This swelling dissatisfaction came to an unexpected head on a camping trip on the Huzzah Creek in southern Missouri one New Year's weekend, a good time and place, I suppose, for resolution.

I was staying in an old log cabin. Without the many distractions of modern life, there wasn't much to do but think, and think I did.

This was a moment of decision. Either I would change my life, or I would squander it. Paradoxical as it may sound, I realized the best way to not squander my life was to sacrifice it for others. To get started, I decided to do a special thing for someone else each day.

This simple decision had a profound effect almost immediately. By focusing my attention on others, I gained a new understanding of people. I could sense when they needed help and could offer it. I could sense when people were hurting and encourage them. In this I gained confidence and a sense of direction. Suddenly I had joy and hope in my life. I did not stop to ask how this transformation was possible, or how I'd managed to set aside sins like an old garment. That understanding would come later. All I knew was I had a new heart.

Enthused once again about life, I landed a great job with IBM back in Massachusetts. The first year included considerable training and lengthy classes at various IBM locations in the Northeast. In June 1974, I attended a one-month manufacturing applications class in Poughkeepsie, New York. During the first week, I discovered all but two of the men were married and that eight of the women were single. Things were clearly starting off well.

I also observed that many of my classmates were interested in tennis. As the newly elected class president (a sign of things to come?), I organized a doubles tournament to break up the intense class schedule. As it turned out, some of the big talkers looked as though they were stalking flies with a fly swatter, but there was one curly-headed young lady who could really smack the ball. I sidled right over and started hitting tennis balls with her. It got to be a habit.

Her name was Lulli, an unusual name by American standards, but not if you were the daughter of two naturalized Norwegian immigrants. That Fourth of July weekend, Lulli and I headed up to northern Vermont to visit my cousin John and go hiking. We chose one of the steepest trails in New England, which climbed the side of Mount Mansfield and ended at the well-named Lake of the Clouds. No false advertising here—when we arrived, a cloud totally obscured the lake.

We headed back down the mountain and were happy to jump into my MGA two-seater parked at the trailhead. We had hiked enough.

As I drove along the twisty roads, Lulli looked over and said, "By the way, happy birthday!" I had forgotten: it was July 5, my birthday. Out of nowhere, a thought entered my mind: *Lulli is my birthday present!* This thought surprised me. Until this moment, I had thought of Lulli as just a friend. More surprising, the thought seemed to come from someplace loftier than my own brain.

Over the next many months, Lulli and I spent most weekends together—white-water canoeing on the Housatonic, sailing a Hobie Cat on Cape Cod Bay, snow skiing when winter came, and of course, playing tennis when we could. Our friendship deepened, and over time, Lulli's love of adventure and her honest, true heart caused me to think she would make a wonderful wife and a great mother.

Months later—January 19, 1975, to be precise—while returning in my little MGA from a wonderful skiing weekend, I leaned over and asked my best friend to join me in a lifelong adventure. She agreed enthusiastically. For both of us, this was the second most important decision of our lives. Five months later, after four straight weeks of rain, the sun blessed our outdoor wedding in the beautiful garden of her parents' 1759 colonial home in Litchfield, Connecticut.

As to that first most important decision, that would come soon enough, but first I had a career decision to make. I had spent four years at IBM. Rewarding as those years were, I never overcame the sense of duty to our family business in Greater St. Louis. For three generations, my family had presided over Laclede Steel, a midsized steel mill that had been founded by my great-grandfather Thomas Russell Akin in 1911.

At the time I returned, my father, Paul, was chairman and CEO. Despite the Carter economy, the firm was a going concern. With my IBM experience, I thought I could make a solid contribution to the success of Laclede. So Lulli and I, along with our newborn son, Wynn, headed west to St. Louis. I would work there for the next three years, overseeing the plant's maintenance operation.

During those years, Lulli and I enrolled in Bible Study Fellowship. I liked the organization for a number of reasons. For one, it was interdenominational. For another, it was not overly "churchy." We simply studied the Bible, the most influential and widely read book in world history. The Bible taught God was not a "force," but a person, and that He offered me a personal relationship with Him. At the time, though, I was not sure if God really would love me. It seemed too good to be true, but I decided to make an appeal, in any case. I knelt down beside my bed and prayed, "God, if You are there, please forgive my sins." (In my day, I had sampled a few.) "I accept that You are the Boss of my life, and I will try to follow and obey You. Jesus, please let me know if You hear my prayer."

I didn't see any lightning or hear any thunder, but I knew in my heart that He had heard and answered my prayer. Now I had a new brain to go with my new heart. I told my parents. They thought the prodigal son had returned. I told my wife. She had made the same commitment a few weeks earlier. *This*, we soon discovered, was the most important decision of our lives and the gateway to an incredible new adventure.

I tell this story because, although I did not know it at the time, my relationship with God would direct me to stand for principle and take the long view of a statesman as opposed to the short-term view of the pragmatist. This difference is now the heart of the conflict within the Republican Party.

Several years later, I believe the Lord took me up on my promise to follow His direction. It started very early one morning when I was not sleeping well, very unusual for me. Lulli rolled over in bed and said, "Maybe God is showing you what He wants you to do." She went back to sleep.

Feeling grumpy, I opened my Bible randomly and found myself at John 21:15–19. This is where Jesus challenges Peter to show his love. "Feed my sheep," says Jesus. That is all He asked, but it was a big ask. He was asking Peter—and, by extension, me—to dedicate his life to furthering the Lord's work. For me, there were other confirmations like this in the days that followed, and they all seemed to be leading me toward "full-time Christian work," though I wasn't quite sure at the time what that meant.

This was not a message I necessarily wanted to hear. I was not eager to go where God seemed to be calling me—Covenant Seminary in St. Louis. Competing with the idea of a hard slog through divinity school was a promising career in business that offered much more in the way of worldly returns. Then too, I had attended engineering school to avoid foreign languages, and I knew seminary included Greek and Hebrew.

For all my internal protests, it was clear that God had plans for me that did not include a big corner office. Despite the sacrifices the Masters of Divinity program would entail, I would follow my conscience. My, how my FIJI fraternity brothers would have been shocked!

Over the next three years, I was booking it. I barely survived Greek and Hebrew, was three times elected class president, and grew in my knowledge of the Bible. All of that, however, did not lead me to believe I had a genuine calling as a minister or a missionary. I was willing to follow God's call and only asked God for the zeal to do it. Ironically, although the job of a minister seemed too political for a person like me, the study of civil government did not.

I trace my interest in American civil government and history to when I was in third grade and my family lived in Concord, Massachusetts. We had moved east so my father could attend Harvard Business School. I was decidedly unhappy about the move. One day, my mother took me down a gravel path lined by boulders that culminated in the Old North Bridge over the Concord River. "It was here, nearly two hundred years earlier," she told me, "the embattled farmers stood / And fired the shot heard round the world.'"[1]

She had the patience to help me memorize Ralph Waldo Emerson's "Concord Hymn" engraved on the brass plaque of the Minuteman statue. Her description of events on and around "the rude bridge that arched the flood" planted a seed of patriotism in a young heart. Love of country does not happen by accident. I still thank my mother for sharing that love with me. (Note to young patriot mothers, as was written on a gravestone in Concord: "Go thou and do likewise!") Now, years later, the seed she planted was beginning to bear fruit.

With seminary just completed, I met with Ed Whitman, the pastor of the East Dennis Community Church of Cape Cod, not far from the site of the *Mayflower* landing. Something of a scholar on matters Puritan, he explained to me over a quiet lunch how those early American Christians approached government.

Pastor Whitman explained that the colonial patriots formed their ideas on government from their Puritan ancestors. The Puritans thought that four different forms of government exist in a society. Governance, they believed, began with the self. A man who could not rule his own desires shouldn't be trusted to rule others. Family was a form of governance as well, forged as it was by a sacred covenant to "have and to hold from this day forward, for better, for worse, for richer, for poorer, in sickness and in health, to love and to cherish, till death us do part." Church government was a third type, and civil government was the fourth. It was civil government that intrigued me and would become my calling.

My discussion with Pastor Ed led to another three years of study on the early history of America from the perspective of an engineer analyzing the faith of our Founders. By this time, my wife had blessed me with four strapping boys. We were poor as church mice, but our home-educated family was full of good humor and love. There was plenty of time for studies, go-carts, mini-bikes, the Marine Club, music, hayrides, the President's Challenge of physical fitness, and lots of home-educated friends.

As I continued my studies, it became obvious that our Founders believed there was a direct connection between faith and freedom. "Our Constitution was made only for a moral and religious people," said John Adams, the second president and a crafter of the Declaration of Independence. "It is wholly inadequate to the governance of any other."[2] Noah Webster, author of the first American English dictionary, felt much the same. Said he, "No truth is more evident to my mind than that the Christian religion must be the basis of any government intended to secure the rights and privileges of a free people."[3]

The great Anglo-Irish statesman and friend of America Edmund Burke may have summed up most succinctly the practical role faith plays in governance: "Society cannot exist unless a controlling power upon will and appetite be placed somewhere," he said, "and the less of it there is within, the more there must be without."[4] From a purely practical perspective, Christianity helps provide that controlling power, but it does more than just control behavior. It introduces into the civil realm the ideas of justice, mercy, and redemption—ideas that have been lacking in the great majority of world cultures, including many, if not most, today. John Adams made this case very well:

> Suppose a nation in some distant Region should take the Bible for their only law Book, and every member should regulate his conduct by the precepts there exhibited! Every member would be obliged in conscience, to temperance, frugality, and industry; to justice, kindness, and charity towards his fellow men; and to piety, love, and reverence toward Almighty God. . . . What a Eutopia, what a Paradise would this region be.[5]

Through my study, I began to see that politics was not about policy. It was about vision. It was about holding in front of yourself, and those you represent, an idea about what America could be and then doing whatever could be done to bring that idea to life. Not all ideas were created equal. Our Founders believed that the things good, noble, and true were worth fighting for. But if good ideas were to triumph over bad, someone had to put them out there. To quote Edmund Burke one more time, "All that is necessary for the triumph of evil is that good men do nothing."[6]

# 4

# AWAKENING:
# 1985

**W**e had been sitting over two hours on metal chairs in a church basement. Normally, such metal chairs would have chilled a vital part of our anatomy and shortened our attention spans. But that winter's eve in 1985, I heard a man speak as if from a fire in his bones, a fire that demanded our complete focus.

The speaker went by the name Tomas Schuman. He was explaining to us in detail how exactly the Soviets went about subverting a culture like our own. In short, they would plant bad ideas like seeds and watch those seeds grow, all too often with the nurturing help of the country's own citizens. They sold these bad ideas by a technique that Schuman called "word pollution," an Orwellian devaluation of a moral tradition by redefining it. For instance, you may think you are pro-life, but to the opposition you are "anti-choice." If you favor traditional marriage, you are said to be a "homophobe" who opposes "marriage equality." If you recognize that men and women are different, you are a "sexist" who denies a woman her "reproductive rights."

The Soviet goal, Schuman explained, was to destroy through language those institutions that serve as a bulwark against socialism:

marriage, the family, the church, and local government. Although the Soviet Union no longer exists, its political heirs have mastered the playbook and are adapting it with great success.

Now, lest you think that this Schuman guy was just some crackpot anticommunist, let me add that his real name is Yuri Alexandrovich Bezmenov. Although in his Soviet days he was alleged to be a "reporter" working primarily in India, Schuman's real boss was the KGB. In 1970, after seven years under the agency's thumb, he courageously defected to the West and became a prolific pro-American writer and lecturer.

What impressed me most that night, what impressed us all, was how positive Schuman remained despite his experiences. He encouraged us to play whatever role we could in defending Western values. He wanted us to work on our leadership skills, develop solidarity groups, prepare for any emergencies, and, regardless of what happened, never forget to "love thy neighbor," the virtue that distinguished us from his former comrades.[1] The fight, he reminded us, was not against bad people, but bad ideas.

As a group, we at the Missouri Roundtable took Schuman's message to heart, and at least three of us were moved to go into politics. Yes, I was among them.

Schuman reaffirmed two critical points: First, as even little children know, there is a great ongoing war in this world—it is between good and evil. Second, our battle is against ideas. We are to judge and discern the core of an idea and vigorously fight the bad ideas. We are, however, to love people. This would become a hallmark of both my campaign style and my personal behavior as an elected office holder. I was diligent to treat my colleagues with respect while vigorously opposing the lies of Liberalism.

# 5

# GETTING POLITICAL:
# 1988

People who fly over Missouri or blow through on I-70 miss a lot. We call it the "Show-Me State," but we could just as well have called it the "Great Rivers State," dominated as it is by the Mississippi and the Missouri. These two rivers and their many tributaries have carved out the most picturesque and topographically diverse state in the Midwest. Missouri is a political paradox. In some ways it is the most typical state in the nation and, in other ways, the least. It is simultaneously a western state, an eastern state, a northern state, and a southern state. Its position at the heart of the westward migration has lent it a history as colorful as the autumn leaves in the Ozarks. The fictional Huck Finn lived here, as did the semi-fictional Jesse James. Lewis and Clark started here. So did the Pony Express. Adding Kansas to the mix, so did the Civil War. During that war, Missouri was divided against itself. Curiously, though, the southern part of the state was the most Union-friendly and the northern the most Confederate-friendly.

This mix of sentiments helped make Missouri America's most reliable predictor of presidential success throughout the twentieth century. In only one election did Missourians not cast the plurality of their votes for the winning candidate. That occurred in 1956, when our citizens just by a hair cast the majority of their votes for Democrat Adlai Stevenson during a year in which the Republican Dwight Eisenhower won by a landslide. I would attribute this otherwise inexplicable outcome to the return of Democrat Harry Truman to Independence, Missouri. In 1952, when Truman was still in Washington, Eisenhower carried the state. After he left the White House, Harry and Bess drove home by themselves to Independence. Can you imagine a president doing that today?

If you look at a county-by-county electoral map from 1956, you will see a distinct pattern that the Democrats would rather not talk about. Although Stevenson ostensibly ran as a liberal, the great majority of counties that he carried were once counties in which the slave trade was legal and in which Jim Crow was still the law of the land.

Now, with slavery gone, these areas still keep their Democratic identity. Many Missouri citizens are pro-life, pro–Second Amendment, pro-God, antitax, and anti–big government, and yet, still vote Democrat. Go figure! As a result of this legacy, Democrats controlled both the Missouri House and Senate when I first ran for office in 1988. Those Republicans who despair of the future can take heart in looking at Missouri's history. In 1988, Democrats held nearly 2-to-1 majorities in both the Missouri House and Senate. The Democrats had controlled the Senate for the last forty years and the House for thirty-four. By 2002, Republicans would control both the House and Senate, and they still do.

I grew up in a family with strong conservative convictions. My folks looked at state politics as a dirty business, run mostly by and for Democratic political bosses of dubious virtue. As I would soon see up close, that family perception was more or less on-target. Although no one in my family had run for office in recent history, I decided to make a run when my local House seat came open in 1988. One of my colleagues from the Missouri Roundtable had run in 1986 and won, and another was about to make a successful bid for still another open seat.

Given the history of Democratic control, I knew that if elected, I would do little more than play defense. Still, I felt the Lord was calling me to run. Lulli was supportive. She reminded me that the price of living in a free country includes rolling up one's sleeves and fixing things that are broken—even if a state rep's salary could barely cover the cost of tennis shoes for our growing family, now four kids strong.

It's one thing to watch politics or to be a volunteer or a staffer. It is a different thing altogether to run for office. I prayed that I would be able to keep a soft heart and a thick hide. My grassroots work through the Roundtable and my in-depth study of civil government had prepared me well for the task. Lulli kept an optimistic outlook and helped where she could. In fact, through her hard work she was able to muster a crowd of three hundred for our campaign kickoff, a sign to all concerned that we would be making a serious bid for the seat.

Because I was running for state representative in a very Republican section of St. Louis County, I would face my toughest opposition in the primary. To try to win the primary, I concentrated on the two types of media that state reps everywhere depend on: yard signs and direct mail. I had hoped to share my larger vision of America with the voters, but as I quickly discovered, few voters in a local race like this one wanted to hear about vision. Plus, it is hard to boil that vision down to a yard sign.

I also resolved to stay away from the mudslinging that characterizes so much of political debate. As Jesus tells us in Matthew, "You have heard that it was said, 'Love your neighbor and hate your enemy.' But I tell you, love your enemies and pray for those who persecute you, that you may be children of your Father in heaven" (5:43–48). Unless I missed something, Jesus offered no exemption for politicians. I resolved to go positive and stay out of the muck. Any candidate can think of negative things to say, but a strong candidate, I believe, should strive for a positive, encouraging vision and let the voters decide which candidate is the stronger one and who represents their views the best. This was also an extension of what I learned at IBM. In IBM, we ignored our competitors and sold our benefits. Now, instead of selling "Big Blue," I would be selling the ideas that make people free, happy, and prosperous.

Years later, some establishment Republican staffers would view me as a weak candidate because I wouldn't "go negative." They misunderstood. I believed it was my job to let citizens know my opponent's belief system and voting record, but I would do so honestly. There is, after all, a commandment not to bear false witness. There is also a commandment not to steal, which prohibition, I would like to remind my Democratic friends, includes votes and yard signs.

As it happened, the summer of 1988 was one of the hottest years, temperature-wise, in recent Missouri memory, and all summers in Missouri are hot. This made walking door to door difficult and planting yard signs almost impossible. Those who have tried to drive a wooden stake into brick-hard ground know what I am talking about. Still, as I would learn in spades in 2012, the physical part of campaigning is a stroll in the park compared to the emotional part.

Our positive vision and hard work paid off. We won the primary comfortably in 1988, and Lulli's grand kickoff must have scared the Democrats out of the race. They failed to put up a candidate, and this "Mr. Smith" was off to Jefferson City. Although "Jeff City" does not impress everyone, it did me. The state capitol rises nearly 250 feet above the bluffs overlooking the Missouri. Its splendid dome dominates the skyline and inspires excellence. Some of my colleagues took the building for granted. I never did. I might have been staying in a third-floor walk-up in a musty old Jeff City mansion, but the capitol architecture reminded me every day of the grandeur of the American Dream.

If I needed humbling, my new role as a freshman state legislator in a minority party gave me all that I could handle and then some. The Democrats thought of us as window dressing. They ignored the fact that voters in our districts had elected us just as their voters had elected them. In spite of our minority status, however, we were able to stop some bills, improve others, and, if nothing else, make their bad bills politically costly on passage.

By playing defense and playing it well, we made them regret their condescension, but it wasn't easy. The first trick for me was to learn the process. Passing laws is occasionally compared to making sausages, something you really don't want to see up close. To have any effect at all, however, I had to become something of a sausage maker. As an engineer, I had an advantage. I understood process. Mine, however, was not exactly a welcome profession in a field dominated by lawyers. At one breakfast meeting, for instance, a prominent Democrat legislator blurted out, "Engineers should not be allowed in politics." I differ with his view and think that it is best to have a legislature representing as many professions as possible. We as legislators faced a wide variety of problems, and the diversity of professions helped us to create better solutions. But mine was not the only opinion. Welcome to Jefferson City.

State legislators remind me at least a little bit of weekend golfers. They love to talk about their game and how they play it, but they forget that not even their golf buddies are interested in the details. So let me just share a few anecdotes from the twelve years I spent in what proved to be a labor of love.

During my first four years, John Ashcroft, a Republican, was the governor. Future US senator Jim Talent was the minority leader in the House. They had agreed with the Democrat State House and State Senate to funnel money to MoDOT, the Missouri Department of Transportation. They were sending this money to do some serious road building. Previously, road bills that needed extra revenue were sent to a vote of the citizens to approve the gas tax increase. This time, however, the Republican and Democratic leadership wanted to bypass the citizenry.

Here was my first test in legislative resolve. The Democratic leadership proposed a significant gas tax hike to pay for this improvement in our state's roads. Ashcroft, a man I like and had come to respect, supported the tax. So did Talent. Needless to say, the big contractors supported it as well. One of them called me the evening before the vote and told me that I *would* vote yes. He obviously did not know me very well. The way I saw it, I worked for someone bigger than the biggest contractor, and the reason I was in politics was to stand for what I thought was right. So when the contractors called, I told them what I told the leadership, "As soon as there is a provision for a public vote, you have my support."

I believed that the public should have a direct say if they were to be asked for more money. I also rejected the notion that government spending "stimulates" the economy. The best test case was the Great Depression. As FDR's treasury secretary, Henry Morgenthau Jr., came to see, the New Deal simply did not deliver.

"We are spending more money than we have ever spent before and it does not work," Morgenthau told a Congressional hearing in 1939. "I want to see this country prosperous. I want to see people get jobs. We have never made good on our promises. . . . I say after eight years of this Administration we have just as much unemployment as when we started . . . and an enormous debt to boot."[1]

The bill passed, but without my vote. This engineer had discovered a helpful principle: put politics aside and just do the right thing. The principle stood me in good stead when my resolve was tested under much greater pressure in the years to come. It's one thing to have Jim Talent or some contractor put the squeeze on you. It is another level of challenge altogether to have US President George Bush or his chief political adviser, Karl Rove, do the same.

Some people believe that public office corrupts leaders, and for this reason they like the idea of term limits. I disagree. I believe that public office does not change people but that it just amplifies their character. Good public servants get a chance to shine. Not-so-good ones get a chance to go awry.

In my first six or seven years in the House, the speaker was a guy named Bob Griffin from western Missouri. He was the kind of Democrat my parents warned me about. He was something of a small-town hero and was politically sly. In the aforementioned gasoline tax issue, Griffin coerced contractor groups to hire a female lobbyist, and she in turn was kicking money back to Griffin. He also used that same lobbyist to work the casino industry for some lively kickbacks. So outsized were Griffin's shenanigans that even the media turned against him.

The *Kansas City Star* ran a series of articles on Griffin, and these provoked federal officials to investigate his dealings. A year after he retired in 1995, the Feds indicted him on a series of bribery and racketeering charges and eventually sentenced him to four years in prison. Conveniently for Griffin, President Bill Clinton commuted his sentence during his infamous orgy of pardons in his last few days in office.

It is a rare day when the mainstream media investigate a Democrat. The routine failure to hold Democrats accountable has the seeming advantage of advancing the Democratic agenda. It has the disadvantage, however, of blocking reform within the party and of allowing out-and-out crooks to achieve high office. Never in my experience, however, have the mainstream media made a Democrat into a pariah over trivia. This is a torture they reserve for Republicans, especially conservatives. I have never minded being held to a higher standard. I do mind not knowing in advance what that standard will be.

At the time, I was way too small potatoes for the media to pay me much attention. In my first reelection campaign, Griffin tried to punish me for my resistance, and I had a tough race; thereafter, I never faced serious opposition. We always had a Democratic opponent, but we always won handily. On the other hand, the 2012 campaign would more than compensate for the relatively easy campaigns that preceded it.

Speaking of Griffin, one bad idea of his that I opposed was state-sanctioned gambling. My research showed that it was not as innocent as it appeared. It addicted ordinary people, led to bankruptcy, destroyed families, and enabled money laundering. For these reasons, I opposed gambling in general and specifically the introduction of casino gambling into Missouri. Unlike the media stereotype of Republicans, I was the one opposing the greedy corporations that exploited poor people. Most of the liberals, however, were in casinos' pockets, so I used to kid them by complaining that I had to do their job for them.

Many people in Missouri were appalled at the way the industry had insinuated itself into our state, a feeling shared even by many who supported gambling. In November 1992, a ballot referendum asked voters whether riverboat casino gaming should be allowed. The gaming industry made a nostalgic appeal to reenergize the Mississippi and the Missouri with historic, old-time riverboats. The electorate approved the measure by approximately 63 percent. No sooner did the referendum pass, however, than the real intent of the industry became clear. Instead of quaint river boats, the gambling industry built giant gambling complexes that were perched on barges with tiny moats around them. These giant complexes were no more capable of navigating the Mississippi than was the Missouri State Capitol.

Legislatively, there was not much I could do about this flagrant violation of the state constitution. So some citizens and I took our case to the courts. In 1996, we filed the case *Akin v. Missouri Gaming Commission* where we argued that the boat-in-a-moat concept violated the provision of the Missouri Constitution that authorized riverboat casinos only on our two major rivers.

As it happened, soon after we filed our lawsuit, I was offered two free tickets to the opening night of the huge multimillion-dollar Hollywood Casino in Maryland Heights. I chose to invite a friend, then working with Casino Watch, the antigambling organization in our state. When we got inside, it was pure glitz. There were local dignitaries everywhere and a half dozen or so TV crews. Nothing if not bold, my friend approached each crew and asked, "Would you like an interview with the guy who's going to shut this casino down?" That guy was me. Soon enough I was explaining our lawsuit to one TV crew after another, and yes, I was doing this inside the casino on opening night!

Management took to us as they would to pickpockets or card counters. Sure enough, I was halfway through my third interview when I noticed three-fingered Igor standing about two feet away from me and about ten inches above me. Wondering how he'd lost those fingers almost caused me to lose my train of thought. We finished the interviews in any case, but I began to wonder if perhaps we had played our hand too aggressively. In concrete overshoes I would be no more capable of floating than this casino.

Some months after the casino's opening, the Missouri Supreme Court ruled in our favor. Chief Justice Duane Benton wrote that the constitution specifically limited gambling to floating facilities solely "over and in contact with the surface of the Mississippi and Missouri Rivers." The court declared the six existing riverboat casinos built in moats unconstitutional.[2] This loss only forced the gambling industry to go back to the voters one more time. Now with thousands of employees and a multitude of political figures and media outlets who were benefiting from their largesse, the industry prevailed again by telling the public that casinos would fund their schools.

Although I fought for "social issues," my most lasting contribution as a state legislator was an "economic issue." I authored a constitutional amendment that required any major tax increase in Missouri to go to a public vote for approval. This legislation was part of the Hancock Amendment to the Missouri Constitution. This bulwark against overtaxation still stands today and slows the spread of state government. As a Republican, I was able to write this amendment because of the Missouri Farm Bureau and the great work of their president, Charles E. Kruse. Interestingly, in the State House as in the US Congress, those who are the most "pro-life" are also the most economically conservative. Conversely, those who are squishy on pro-life, or are pro-abortion, are the most economically liberal.

Of course, we also dealt with abortion in my time in the Missouri House. The 1973 Supreme Court decision *Roe v. Wade* rests on three pernicious lies, which I cover in chapter 17.

I think abortion is a huge problem for America. If it is wrong to murder innocent people and if the unborn are people, then abortion easily trumps slavery as the greatest moral evil in American history.

Throughout my career I wished I could have done more to end this evil, but as a minority legislator, the best I could do was play defense. We played a lot of defense.

Abortion advocates looked for any angle to advance their unholy cause, and they would often cloak their efforts with the most innocent-seeming cover schemes.

One such cover scheme came in the package of a bill allegedly designed to increase the number of school nurses. This was a hard bill to oppose under any circumstances, so I offered a simple amendment, namely that school nurses would not be able to counsel students about abortions or refer them to abortionists. With a little arm-twisting, lots of prayer, and support from most Republicans and several genuinely pro-life Democrats, the amendment passed. No sooner did my amendment pass than its Democratic sponsor pulled the bill. In doing so, he and his allies tipped their hand. They did not care about school nurses. They cared about increasing access to abortion.

We fought this bill every year. In fighting it I made a serious enemy out of then Democrat governor Mel Carnahan. I recall one instance where my pastor went to a Cardinals' baseball game. He saw Carnahan in the broadcast booth and introduced himself. He then innocently told Carnahan that he was a friend of mine. At the mention of my name, Carnahan turned beet red, spun on his heel, and abruptly walked away.

What Governor Carnahan didn't understand was that abortion was antithetical to all that America has stood for. Unlike any other country, America was established on the conviction that our Creator intended to bless all of His children with life. That same sentence in our Declaration goes on to assert that it is the purpose of civil government to protect not only life, but liberty and the pursuit of happiness as well. It follows, therefore, that a government that doesn't protect life has failed in its most important duty. This belief is still ingrained in many Americans who daily make great personal sacrifices, even risking their lives, to protect life in the nation they love.

# 6

# GOING TO WASHINGTON: 2000

The drumbeat was echoing through the streets, "Akin's too conservative to win the general election for Congress." There are others who are better than I, who have heard that drumbeat—Ronald Reagan comes to mind—so I cannot complain too much. Still, it would be nice if our moderate allies would put this bit of conventional non-wisdom in mothballs for a while.

The drumbeat started in 1999 when it became obvious that our local congressman, Republican Jim Talent, was eyeing the governorship. This meant that the seat he held in the US House of Representatives would be up for grabs, and the Republicans would have an edge in securing it. I was not anyone's obvious choice to take his place, not even mine. As a state representative with six kids and no major-league piggy bank from which to pull, the idea of winning a congressional seat seemed altogether daunting.

Over the years, I had learned how to approach a major decision of this type, and for me, it started in prayer. After turning to God, I turned to Lulli. If she would not support the race, I wouldn't run. It was that simple. Lulli knows me as well as I know myself, and she recalled some encouraging signs: my willingness to stand up to Carnahan, my tenacity in taking on the casino industry, and, perhaps most important, my unflagging dedication to her and my six children despite the temptations that elected office held. She also mentioned a small, seemingly insignificant incident that had occurred several years before.

One lunchtime in Jefferson City, just after the State House adjourned, I decided to grab a bite at the small restaurant in the Capitol basement. Standing in front of the glass partition, I ordered a cheeseburger with lettuce and tomato, but no onions. I explained, "My wife doesn't like it when I eat onions before coming home." The young lady behind the partition joked, "Yeah, onions are okay other times of the week for the other women." Sensing an opportunity to sell a good idea, I paused and said, "I think just one woman is enough for a man." She froze for about twenty seconds, then responded softly and sadly, "I wish my man believed that."

Lulli recalled this story. She was mindful of the very high incidence of divorce among legislators and believed that, with God's blessing, our marriage could withstand the challenges of Washington, DC. Yes, with God's blessing and Lulli on board, I had a sense of peace that it was okay to run. I understood, of course, that there were no guarantees. This was a calculated risk.

On paper, I was a pure long shot. I did, however, have some things going for me. First, I had a twelve-year record as a proven conservative legislator. This would get the attention of many serious conservatives. Second, it was a crowded and diverse field, which could play to a candidate with loyal supporters. Third, we had been building a database of conservative Republicans for several years under the able care of Vivian and Rodger Young, a couple of very dear friends who are the most skillfully competent data managers/programmers one could ever meet. Ours was much better than the party database, as it allowed us to target possible supporters more accurately. Fourth, I had a good handle on America's founding principles. This knowledge proved invaluable in talks and debates. It's helpful to know what you believe and why.

On the other side of the equation, beyond my lack of funding, were the four other serious candidates queuing up in the Republican primary. The most formidable was Gene McNary. A former prosecutor, McNary had served four terms as St. Louis county executive and three years as head of the Immigration and Naturalization Service under the senior President George Bush. He had enough name identification to have run for US Senate against incumbent Tom Eagleton and come very close to winning. If that were not enough, he was capable of writing much bigger checks to his own campaign than I was. In summing up the race, one Beltway pundit dismissed me as a "third-tier candidate."[1]

What the Beltway thought about my candidacy had never much troubled me. I had prayed, turned to my family for support, and roughed out a campaign plan. As I saw it, my job was to assemble our team, give it our all, and trust God for the outcome. For me, it was to be up or out.

Those who have run for office know that campaigning is an emotional roller coaster. In the morning you start high and optimistic, and you can have half a dozen ups and downs by bedtime. One evening, exhausted, I sat in our large living room. On an angled ceiling, Lulli had stretched a large "AKIN FOR U.S. CONGRESS" banner, lest it wrinkle when folded. As I gazed up at the sign, I asked myself, *Is this some terrible joke? Am I kidding myself about Congress, or do we have a real chance?* That would not be the last time I asked the question.

Most Republican elected officeholders tend to fall into one of two categories. Some place a premium on getting along with others. They tend to be pragmatic and moderate. Others are principled and willing to fight for right. When confronted with a difficult issue, the pragmatists avoid it entirely or cooperate with others to smooth out differences. They want to work with everyone and be enemies to no one. On many issues, these public servants do a decent enough job. Compromise is a good and necessary part of the political process. In contrast, the second group is motivated by principle. These conservatives are willing to lead on tough issues, regardless of vote outcomes. They do not compromise on core beliefs, because they understand who we are as a state or nation and hold their ground.

What I have discovered over the years is that principled consistency attracts support from citizens who care about the political system. They expect bad politics from the Democrats, but it truly dismays them when the Republicans they voted for abandon or soften their position on a key issue. So although my initial name recognition was much less than McNary's, the passion for my campaign among those who did know me was much more intense. It is not that they thought I was a great man, but rather that I was a good man who shared their values and was not about to betray them: they had seen my consistency and commitment against pressure in school nurses bills, in road bills, in the casino battle, and more.

About seven years before the primary, Michael Weisskopf of the *Washington Post* stirred up a hornet's nest when he described the Christian right as "largely poor, uneducated, and easy to command."[2] Bad enough was Weisskopf's casual bigotry. Worse was his flat-out ignorance. Every serious poll of political knowledge done in recent years shows conservatives to be the best informed of the electorate. It stands to reason that conservatives are informed because to adopt the principles we've adopted, we've had to assess and then reject the please-yourself mainstream philosophy that the media disseminate 24/7.

As to their wealth, the head of a conservative household, if not retired, is almost always employed. Few among the Christian right are dependent on government. If they are seemingly less affluent than the average liberal, it is because the mother works in the home, and the family has more children. These children are the ones who will be funding Social Security for retired liberals. As to the "easy to command" part, are you kidding, Mr. Weisskopf? It is not conservatives who are registered to vote at casinos and rock concerts or who are driven to the polls in buses.

If we'd had the money to run our one TV commercial more often, we might have pulled away from the field, but we did not.

So we had to slug it out throughout the steamy summer of 2000 heading into an August primary—making calls, pounding yard signs, sending mailers, and always, inevitably, asking for support in whatever form it might come. By the way, if I use *we* in talking of the campaign instead of *I*, it is not due to any false modesty. As anyone who has ever worked on a campaign can tell you, it's a team sport.

Happily, my children were coming of age, and they would become key players on the team. In the 2000 election, Perry was off to summer training at the Naval Academy, but Micah, who was just seventeen, emerged as the campaign's go-to guy on all things electronic—phones, computers, you name it. He was indispensable. Another noteworthy addition to our team was Amanda Carman. She, too, came from a large home-educating family and was a wizard at organization. Amanda impressed us all, but Perry most especially—so much so that she is now Mrs. Perry Akin and the mother of six of our wonderful grandchildren. You never know what good can come out of a campaign.

Although no candidate likes to make fund-raising calls, principled conservatives have an advantage. We sell the same set of principles to all comers. Moderates tend to negotiate based on the needs of the person called. My supporters were Reaganites, mostly from the western part of the district. McNary's clustered in the well-to-do suburbs in the district's eastern part. I may have been getting fewer dollars per donor, but I was almost keeping even, and I was spending less.

I tried hard to stay positive and focused. I imagined my campaign as an auto race and my opponents not as fellow drivers I had to beat, but as the orange cones I had to get around to win. I did not want the campaigning to get personal. I respected my primary opponents and understood that, for all our differences, we were still allies in a greater cause, especially come general election days!

After the polls closed on that August primary day, at least 150 of our friends and supporters gathered at my parents' home for an un-air-conditioned cliffhanger of a night. It had been a long day for me, as I had been handing out literature and meeting voters outside a polling place starting at 6 a.m. Others in the room were just as tired. As the results trickled in, depending on which part of the district was reporting, the mood shifted from elation to despair, back to elation and back to despair. It was that close. I don't know what they were doing at McNary headquarters, but we were praying.

Seeking the strength to deal with either outcome, I retreated to my closet/office and started reciting Psalm 139, which we, as a family, had put to music and memorized. As I recited the concluding lines—"Search me, God, and know my heart; test me and know my anxious thoughts. See if there is any offensive way in me, and lead me in the way everlasting" (vv. 23–24 NIV)—I heard a wonderfully spontaneous roar come from the crowd down the hall, and I knew it could only mean one thing. We won! And by only fifty-six votes!

I made my way back to the crowd in a stupor. People were laughing and crying, patting me on the back and high-fiving me. There have been a lot of low moments in my political career— one of those made my name a negative byword around the world—but the highs really do compensate, especially when shared with the people you love.

The general election was no cakewalk. My opponent, state senator Ted House, was a pro-life Democrat who was aggressively positioning himself as just that. As glad as I was that he chose the side of life, it confused me then and still confuses me now how anyone could embrace the cause of life and still align himself with a party that champions abortion. My opponent's position confused more than a few people in the pro-life community.

My life on the campaign trail was improved because I now had the support of the Republican Party, both state and national. Senator Kit Bond also lent me his very competent staffer to manage my campaign. In the primary, I had been my own campaign manager.

As I quickly learned, no gift comes without strings. The Beltway Republicans hoped to remake me in their image. One place where they thought a makeover was most needed was my

TV ad. In this ad, much to their consternation, the word *God* was mentioned, not just once but three times. They even proposed negotiating the mention of *God* down to once, but this, I told them, was not a subject for negotiation.

After some prayerful contemplation, I concluded that, if I lost the election because I stood up for what I believed, I was meant to lose. I refused to change the ad. We won the general election with more than 55 percent of the vote. "Mr. Smith" was on his way to Washington.

# 7

# STATE OF THE UNION: 2001

"**M**r. Speaker, Mr. Vice President, Members of Congress," said our new president, George W. Bush, good-naturedly, as was his habit, "It's a great privilege to be here to outline a new budget and a new approach for governing our great country. I thank you for your invitation to speak here tonight. I know Congress had to formally invite me, and it could have been a close vote." The president was referring indirectly to the harrowing vote count in Florida that finally secured him his job. We all laughed, at least on our side of the aisle. Getting there had been not easy for many of us, me included.

But there I was, in the crowded House Chamber, a Member of Congress, part of the greatest deliberative body in the history of the planet. Around me there were the representatives like myself, senators, the Supreme Court justices, the president, the vice president, and the ubiquitous TV cameramen. The Capitol building itself lent an air of majesty to the proceedings. I had become a witness to history, and finally I had a moment to catch my breath and take stock of what all had happened to me. It was genuinely exciting.

The past two months had been a blur. When I arrived in December,

Republican leadership held a series of orientation and policy classes for first-termers like myself: Darrell Issa, Mike Pence, Eric Cantor, and others. The classes ran five days a week and just about all day. That would not have been a burden in itself, but I was also expected to hire a staff at the same time, both for my Washington office and my Missouri district office. That would not have been onerous either if I'd had an actual office and a secretary, but all that I had at that point was a cubicle and a BlackBerry. The life of a rookie is never easy, no matter what you are a rookie in.

As the session got rolling, I was thankful to have been elected as the Republican class vice president. I was also thankful for getting a chance to serve on the Armed Services Committee, my first choice of committee. I got the immediate impression that it would take years to get up to speed on the US military. I was right. It did. We were also warned that our first six months were the most dangerous politically, given that a bad first impression can shorten or end one's public service.

I prayed in particular that I would avoid contracting that mysterious ailment known locally as "Potomac fever." In its more virulent forms, it has been known to amplify pride, cloud judgment, and weaken courage. The "fever" leads to poor legislative decisions and some shabby moral ones as well. Divorce rates are high in Congress. Infidelity rates are incalculable, and misbehavior always takes a toll, occasionally a very high toll. There is no known cure for Potomac fever, short of some career-ending scandal.

In my first year on the job, Gary Condit, a seven-term Democrat from California, got caught in a mess of his own making. His casual affair with an intern thirty years his junior became a national scandal when the young woman, Chandra Levy, turned up missing. Although it later emerged that Condit had nothing to do with her disappearance, his evasiveness about his relationship with her made him look guilty. Tragically, Levy had been murdered. The killer was an illegal immigrant who had already been convicted of two other attacks on women in that same park. If you have not heard about his arrest or conviction, it is because the media do not like to report stories that reflect badly on their agenda, in this case the dark side of illegal immigration. The dark side of Congress? That's a different story.

I had not been in Congress long when I faced the first challenge all new members face: choosing between loyalty to your party or commitment to your principles. Three days after being sworn in, President Bush proposed his signature piece of legislation, an education bill known as "No Child Left Behind" (NCLB). Although the bill called for rigorous testing, with the states designing the tests, the federal Department of Education would manage the whole process. In addition, the bill included significant additional funding for the Department of Education.

In my campaign, I had promised to work to eliminate that department. I could find no logic to federal control of what was clearly a local prerogative. I wasn't about to empower the Department of Education by supporting this legislation, no matter how well intended.

Built into NCLB were a whole series of mandates. States had to do X; schools had to do Y; if the schools or states failed, the federal government would do Z. I had a particular problem with a yardstick called "Adequate Yearly Progress." The so-called AYP—they love initials in DC—was supposed to measure results and punish those school districts that failed to measure up. Those of us who believe in limited constitutional government objected not just to the inefficiency and expense of the Department of Education judging progress, but more importantly, to the loss of local control. Why join the PTA or run for the school board if the ultimate decisions about your child's education would be made thousands of miles away by people who won't even take your phone calls?

While I disagreed with the president on this particular bill, I never doubted his good intentions. George Bush, as president, was in many ways a great leader. He was honorable, good natured, and had the courage and ability to confront and solve problems. I had a lot of respect, too, for Denny Hastert, the low-key Speaker of the House, a fine man and an able leader. I had a good relationship as well with House whip Tom DeLay. Given his role, not everyone liked DeLay, but he was a genuine conservative and a shrewd politician.

All that said, the NCLB legislation was coauthored by Senator Ted Kennedy. Should that not have told the Republicans something? Whenever I heard him or his colleagues talk about the "Republican war on women," I had to bite my tongue. I could only imagine how the Kopechne family felt when they heard those words.

More problematically, Kennedy was a self-described "progressive." They call people "progressive" because they, well, "progress." Once they get their hooks into a program, they instinctively want to grow it and expand their own power. In this regard, Democrats are as strategically consistent as a magnetic compass. Democratic bills with few exceptions do three things: first, cost the taxpayer more money; second, increase the size and power of the government; and third, as a consequence, reduce our freedom. True to form, when the Obama people took over NCLB, they ran it pretty much any way they wanted. Dismayed by the results, the Republicans in the House finally voted to overhaul the program in 2013.

If we Republicans have a chronic weakness, it is our belief that if we compromise, the Democrats will meet us halfway. The Democrats don't have to. The media have their back, and too many of their supporters would rather beat Republicans than work for the betterment of the country. To the degree that Democratic activists have political principles, those principles can change when it suits the strategy of their party leaders. Witness, for instance, President Obama's evolving position on same-sex unions. By contrast, conservatives know what their principles are. Try cajoling our people out of those principles, and you will cajole yourself out of Congress quicker than you can say, "Arlen Specter."

I was expecting House leaders to lean on me for my vote on NCLB, but they did not have to. They knew they had plenty of votes in the bag. Only forty-five of us voted against NCLB. Nearly four hundred voted for it. Let's see: The program spent a lot more taxpayer dollars. It increased the size and power of the government. And it took away parents' freedom to oversee their children's education. That would explain the high level of Democrat support. But what explained Republican support? It seemed to me that in the spirit of compromise, Republicans had betrayed the principle of limited government. I can see compromise on procedure, but never on principle.

While there are occasional examples of members of Congress who behave badly, most work very hard over very long hours. Let me give you a feel for a typical legislative day. Mine started very early with a reading from my Bible and with prayer. Some days, I would go to the gym for a workout and then be off to an 8 a.m. breakfast meeting somewhere on the Hill, usually with someone who added to my knowledge base—a political leader, a Supreme Court justice, an editorial writer, or a subject-matter expert. Afterwards, I took a very fast walk to a committee hearing, accompanied by a knowledgeable staffer who, while we walked, suggested questions for the witness in addition to the questions I had of my own. As a freshman, I did not get to ask many questions, but I always wanted to be prepared. From the hearing room, I rushed to the Capitol for a vote, looking about for colleagues I could recruit to cosponsor a bill of my own or to plan some other legislative maneuver. Between votes, I headed back to the Capitol's stately Rayburn Building to meet with con-stituents. After the final vote, I hurried to the committee hearing to get in a question, or I headed off to another committee hearing going on simultaneously.

If possible, I met with various groups back at my office, tried to catch a sandwich for lunch on the fly, then headed off to another meeting, and finally hustled back to the office for a radio interview—but, oops! They were now calling votes—so I took the interview on the cell phone as I walked over to vote. Sometimes, in the evenings, if there were no meetings, and if I had not hit the gym early in the morning, I opted to skip dinner and made my way to the gym or, better still, in good weather, went for a run around the Capitol Mall.

No matter what, I called home and then ended my day with a prayer, God willing, by midnight.

I sometimes thought of myself as a Formula One driver, forever shifting gears as I moved from one wildly diverse topic to another, usually at fifteen- to twenty-minute intervals. One minute I could be talking about weapons of mass destruction in Iraq at an Armed Services Committee meeting. The next minute I could be talking about the tax policies that could restore the economy, and the next moment I could be taking a group of pastors or schoolchildren on a tour of the Capitol.

Until they win that second election, members of Congress are vulnerable. Given the closeness of my primary win, I had to start raising money almost immediately to discourage a primary challenge. This meant a lot of phone calls, which took a lot of discipline because there was nothing fun about asking people for money, and little time into which to squeeze those calls. Complicating matters, according to the law I had to be outside of a government building to make such fund-raising calls.

One oasis amid this controlled chaos was our Thursday morning congressional Bible study. About twenty or thirty of us, Democrats and Republicans, with an occasional foreign dignitary, would meet over breakfast for prayer, song, Bible reading, and the sharing of a personal testimony from a fellow or former congressman. In time, I assumed the role of designated "song-meister," picking the hymns, leading the singing, and occasionally accompanying on my guitar.

The members' favorite was the bluegrass classic "Are You Washed in the Blood?" I accompanied the song on my guitar, and Congressman Jim Cooper added his banjo. It's a kicker of a tune, and it woke everyone up the mornings we played it. If you don't know this hymn, google the title and "Alan Jackson," a country star who is not afraid to share his faith.

Most political activity in DC drove congressmen from the two parties apart, but the weekly members' prayer breakfast exerted a good and unifying influence. In addition, some of the personal testimonies were incredible and unforgettable. We usually set politics aside during these breakfasts, and most of us left feeling more committed to doing our very best as public servants.

The Founders were well aware of the value of breakfasts like these. Almost to a person they believed that faith shaped the manners of individuals and society in general and was a building block of freedom.

This theme recurred repeatedly in their writings, George Washington's included. "And let us with caution indulge the supposition, that morality can be maintained without religion," said Washington in his farewell address. "Whatever may be conceded to the influence of refined education on minds of peculiar structure, reason and experience both forbid us to expect that national morality can prevail in exclusion of religious principle."[1]

Often claimed as one of their own by "freethinkers," our third president, Thomas Jefferson, had no illusions about what was necessary to make government work. "God who gave us life, gave us liberty," he pointedly warned us in his *Notes on the State of Virginia*. "And can the liberties of a nation be thought secure when we have removed their only firm basis, a conviction in the minds of the people that these liberties are of the Gift of God?"[2] These words are engraved on the Jefferson Memorial in Washington, DC. Were a teacher to say these words now at a graduation ceremony, he or she might get fired. That makes no sense to me either.

Among many others, Jedediah Morse, who was the "Father of American Geography" and the actual father of telegraph inventor Samuel Morse, made the faith/freedom connection quite clear in a 1799 speech:

> To the kindly influence of Christianity we owe that degree of civil freedom, and political and social happiness which mankind now enjoys. In proportion as the genuine effects of Christianity are diminished in any nation, either through unbelief, or the corruption of its doctrines, or the neglect of its institutions, in the same proportion will the people of that nation recede from the blessings of genuine freedom, and approximate the miseries of complete despotism.[3]

Just as we members of the congressional Bible study saw an improvement in all our attitudes, in a larger sense, our Founders believed faith a prerequisite to political freedom. As we are seeing today in America, where faith fades, so does freedom.

# 8

# SEPTEMBER 11, 2001

I f you talk to anyone who was on the East Coast that sunny Tuesday in September, they will tell you just how crisp and clear that day was, a promise of an autumn just around the corner. I had been in Washington about eight months, not including my many trips back to St. Louis. I was staying at the time in a small basement room in the home of my chief of staff, Jack Bailey, in Alexandria, Virginia, not far from the Pentagon. I got up, exercised, drove in, and arrived at my office on the fifth floor of the Cannon Building around eight in the morning.

About an hour later, I heard an excited conversation in the outer office. Curious, I walked out and saw a group of my staffers huddled around the television set, speculating on what they were watching. A few minutes earlier, at 8:46 a.m., American Airlines Flight 11 from Boston had flown into the North Tower of the World Trade Center. At 9:03 a.m. all thought of accident vanished when United Airlines Flight 175 flew into the Trade Center's South Tower. This was war. A half hour later, that war came to DC, when American Airlines Flight 77 flew into the Pentagon.

While I would like to assure the reader that we were well prepared for an attack like this and immediately went to our assigned battle stations, that did not happen. Our building security personnel had no idea what to do or what to tell us. We were as disconnected from information as any office worker anywhere in the city. If it were not for the television, we would have known close to nothing at all.

When I saw the smoke billowing from the Pentagon, I saw my first responsibility as getting my office staff clear of the DC area. If the terrorists could attack the Pentagon, they could just as easily attack the Capitol. In fact, United Flight 93 was almost assuredly heading to Washington when the passengers bravely wrested control of the plane from the hijackers over western Pennsylvania. Once I was sure my staff had left, Jack Bailey and I drove back past the Pentagon to his house and got through just before authorities closed down I-395. I would have liked to have stopped and helped, but the first responders had no use for well-intentioned amateurs, even members of Congress.

That day passed for me in as much a fog as it did for most Americans, no matter where they lived. Communication by cell phone was impossible, but I got in touch with Lulli to assure her I was okay. I also got through to my son Perry who was at school and talked to my other five children back in St. Louis. There was something about that day that made us love our loved ones all the more.

I reached out to my constituents as well. At first I thought my role was to provide them with information, but what they really wanted was advice on how to process all the information that we were being inundated with. In other words, how should we feel about our lives, about the attack, about our country, and about our very future?

One powerful and vivid impression I took away from that day was how much Americans value not only their own lives but also the lives of others. I saw this value of life up close when a group of my colleagues and I took the train up to New York City shortly afterward and toured Ground Zero. I began to get a real sense of the horror of it all as I saw the wreckage of the twin towers and the scores of surrounding buildings damaged or destroyed by the jet fuel and flying debris. And yet, I also saw how God was in charge—out of the more than 250,000 people who were daily in the towers, fewer than three thousand died. There are so many incredible stories.

In the midst of the carnage, though, people had erected a number of block-long plywood billboards on which loved ones had posted pictures of those who had died or were missing. It was a drizzly day, and the rain had misted the plastic protecting the images. As I looked through those covers, my heart began to catch up with my head. I began to see the soul of this story.

The many different photographs, some black and white, others in color, touched all of us who saw them. I remember one particular picture of a man and his dog, another of a mother and daughter, another still of a happy family posing at an anniversary. I thought of what their September 11 morning must have been like: a tender meeting of the eye before going out the front door, the gentle brush of hair and a quick kiss, a hasty and final good-bye. This was not so much a saga of airplanes and buildings; it was a terribly poignant human drama.

Many of those who died, I saw, died trying to save the life of a perfect stranger. These were otherwise "ordinary" Americans who had shown the hearts of heroes in risking their own lives for the lives of their fellow citizens. I imagined that these people had behaved on September 11 the same selfless way they had been practicing in small ways for many years. They had been schooling themselves to do the courageous thing, and when crunch time came, they were ready. Their memory is a living memorial to true patriots who "more than self their country loved, and mercy more than life." The looters and exploiters, I suppose, also behaved as they had practiced, trying to get something for nothing. We chose to forget that they were ever our countrymen.

I found the story of John Abruzzo particularly moving. Wheelchair-bound, he was working on the sixty-ninth floor of the North Tower when the plane struck above him. Although the elevators weren't working, his coworkers refused to abandon him. Taking turns, they carried him down all sixty-nine flights, lifted him through the lobby-strewn rubble, and out through a broken window. They had just gotten him away from the building when it collapsed behind them.[1]

No one but Abruzzo and a few others know the name of those ten coworkers, but on September 11, they and other patriots acted out their gut belief that life is a precious gift, one worthy of self-sacrifice. The Declaration puts the protection of life first, and so did they. In the fury of that day, these heroes probably didn't reflect on the human instinct to protect life, let alone the extension of that protection to the unborn, but if they had, they would have seen how antithetical abortion is to everything for which America stands. This was a message I would share in the years to come, including on that Friday I spoke with Charles Jaco.

September 11 provided something of a wake-up call for all of us. The obvious lesson was that America could not endure if we refused to distinguish good ideas from bad ideas. The fact that liberals had "Coexist" bumper stickers on their Priuses failed to protect them from people who had no intention of coexisting with those who did not share their ideas. And some ideas, we saw all too clearly, were too evil to coexist with the core values that most Americans hold dear.

In the following nine months, there was unusual harmony in America, perhaps because we recognized we had a common foe. But there was another effect at work. It seemed that Liberalism had taken a body blow. It had been confronted with undiluted evil, something liberals find awkward to acknowledge. This is why liberals always want to cut national defense—they aren't so sure we need it.

On September 20, I joined my fellow members of Congress, both House and Senate, for a historic moment in the House Chamber. I suspect that this chamber had not experienced such emotion since 1963 or perhaps 1941 or even 1865. "In the normal course of events, presidents come to this chamber to report on the state of the union," said President Bush. "Tonight, no such report is needed; it has already been delivered by the American people."

Our opponents in the Democratic Party and their allies in the media had convinced themselves on the basis of some scattered bits of evidence that President Bush was an awkward bumbler not up to the task of leading the nation. They were deceiving themselves. I saw the president up close for eight years, and I never saw him give a bad speech. On this evening, he was magisterial. What distinguished him from the presidents who came immediately before and after him was that he did not have to tell you that he cared. You could sense it in every fiber of his being. Said the President when speaking of our national resolve:

> We have seen it in the courage of passengers who rushed terrorists to save others on the ground. Passengers like an exceptional man named Todd Beamer. And would you please help me welcome his wife, Lisa Beamer, here tonight?
> We have seen the state of our union in the endurance of rescuers working past exhaustion. We've seen the unfurling of flags, the lighting of candles, the giving of blood, the saying of prayers in English, Hebrew and Arabic. We have seen the decency of a loving and giving people who have made the grief of strangers their own. My fellow citizens, for the last nine days, the entire world has seen for itself the state of our union, and it is strong.[2]

The next twelve years would test that strength, especially the last five of those twelve.

# 9

# TOUGH DECISIONS

**P**resident George Bush expected loyalty. That is the kind of leader he was. He was also an honest, hardworking, patriotic man and a good manager. He set priorities and stuck to them. But as much as I admired him, I was not about to vote with him when I thought he was wrong. That is the American spirit of freedom of conscience.

The divide between the principled conservatives in the House and the pragmatic ones reached a head during the 2003 debate on Medicare Part D, sometimes called the Medicare prescription drug benefit. As a way of wooing older voters and showing the "compassionate" side of conservatism, the White House initiated this legislation. Bush would call the measure "the greatest advance in health care coverage for America's seniors since the founding of Medicare."[1]

Speaker Denny Hastert formally introduced the bill in the House on June 25, 2003, as H.R. 1. There was a good deal of debate about the plan, most of it on the technicalities of whether it would benefit drug manufacturers and insurance companies more than it would the recipients. But for me, these arguments missed the point. The real issue was whether it expanded the role of the federal government. As a constitutional conservative, I objected to that expansion on both practical and philosophical grounds. On philosophical grounds, as the saying goes, a government powerful enough to give you everything you want is powerful enough to take away everything you have. On practical grounds, have we known the federal government to run any program better than the private sector does?

To be a team player, I voted to allow the bill to go to conference, but I knew it had to come back, and if what came back looked anything like what we sent to conference, I was prepared to vote against it. When the bill did come back, it was even more liberal than when it left the House. Upon its return, leadership checked with the individual members, a process known as "whip check." House leaders were not about to let a bill with this kind of political weight be voted on without knowing if it had enough support to pass. The whip check let them know where the members stood, and this member promptly told them NO.

The House leaders only initiated the whip check after weeks of persuasion that included conference meetings in which "experts" sang the bill's praises, exhortations from the committee chairmen and the House, and finally, appeals to the old-school spirit. "We have to stick together as a team," I was told in one variation or another multiple times. Leadership was not above calling some of our better donors and leaning on them to lean on us. The day of the vote I got a call from Karl Rove, who was riding with the president on Air Force One. "Sorry, Karl," I told him, "I'm a no." Later that evening, President Bush himself called. He was courteous, forceful, and to the point. He wanted my vote. I explained my opposition and politely held my ground.

Knowing they were still short on votes, House leaders planned a nighttime vote. That way they could hold the vote open as long as they needed and, through peer pressure and sleep deprivation, wear down the resistance of at least a few of the twenty-five or so of us still holding out. For hours my friends bombarded me. One of the arguments they used was pragmatic: "If we don't pass this bill, then we will be forced to pass a much worse Democratic bill." You can bet I did a lot of praying for wisdom that night. Near dawn, I was handed a cell phone and asked, "Do you want to talk to the president?" I took the call. The president was firm. I told him my vote was captive to my conscience; I was still a no. He may not have been pleased, but I think he understood. That was the hardest vote of my twenty-four-year political career.

My conservative friends were under similar pressure. The most public of these exchanges involved Rep. Nick Smith of Michigan. In return for a change in vote from nay to yea, he claimed to have been offered "substantial and aggressive campaign support" for his son's bid to replace him in the House. He assumed that meant financial support, and he was likely right in his assumption. To his credit, Smith refused to be bought. Those who saw the Steven Spielberg movie *Lincoln* learned that this is the way legislation has frequently been made. Leadership preys on the "moderates," those without fixed principles, sometimes, as in the case of the antislavery amendments, in pursuit of a good cause.

For whatever reason, a handful of Republicans switched their vote at the last minute and allowed the bill to pass. I was not among them. I knew my constituents did not want to hear how the Republican Party was expanding entitlements, even if we expanded them more responsibly than Democrats did. That is not why my supporters sacrificed to send me to Congress. My primary responsibility was to vote for what was in the best interests of the people I served—not to appease Republican leadership or President Bush, as much as I respected him.

I often hear the phrase "The Republican Leaders" or "The Republican Establishment" as though a small handful of people decide how all Republicans are to vote and what policies they are supposed to support. When conservatives talk about "The Republican Establishment," they are referring to a group of Beltway RINOs (Republicans In Name Only). Some who would be included in such a group are Mitch McConnell, John Cornyn, John McCain, Lindsey Graham, John Boehner, Karl Rove, and Roy Blunt from

Missouri. Conservatives are fully aware that most of the Super PACs are closely tied to the decisions of this group. All who must face elections also recognize that major contributions are a must and that repeated rejection of the establishment's orders can be costly.

There is no question that these RINOs wield considerable power and control, but it is not yet complete. There are many in the US House and the US Senate who refuse to yield and will not vote for poor or bad laws. I had the president and Speaker asking for my votes, but they had no power to make me vote any particular way. In Europe, you vote with your party. In America, you can vote with your conscience. Yes, there are people who can influence how a member of Congress votes, but there is no decision-making cabal that can compel behavior. Try as hard as some influential Republicans did in 2012, they could not force me out of the Senate race. They could—and sometimes did—make my life miserable, but the people of Missouri held the ultimate power.

I was convinced, and still am, that the Republican House in 2004 and 2005 was making a tactical mistake and taking the wrong message to our core supporters. We were bragging about how "compassionate" we were, but with their tax dollars. Instead, we should have been telling them about our conservative legislative successes. I made this point in Republican conference meetings to the leadership and other members of Congress. On a foam board, I listed our accomplishments thus:

**Ergonomics repealed**
Americans saved billions of dollars and thousands of jobs

**Missile defense**
Ronald Reagan's vision becoming reality

**UN "Kyoto Accord" dumped**
Would have greatly increased energy costs and crippled some American industries

**Tax cuts**
Marginal rate reduction, death tax, marriage penalty, child care deduction increased, reduced dividend and capital gains tax

**Economy**
From recession to best quarter past 6 months—500,000 jobs

**Abortion**
Ban on partial-birth abortion, "Mexico City Policy," conservative judges, UN

**Educational Choice**
Approved for the Washington, DC school system

**Defense**
Restored funding for defense (25%) and rebuilding human intelligence

**2nd Amendment**
Sunset expired on "Assault Weapons Ban"

**American Values**
God-given right to "Life, Liberty & Pursuit of Happiness" upheld through war on terror

My point was we should have been selling our conservative accomplishments, not that we had expanded an entitlement. In addition, there was also a great number of other conservative bills passed in the House, but because we didn't have sixty Republican senators, the bills—with the exception of the tax cuts—all died. Our base never learned the many good things we had done. For years afterward, conservatives told me, "When the Republicans ran Congress, they got nothing done." The fact is America would be much better off if we had had the sixty votes in the Senate. The media breathed scarcely a word about obstructionist Democrats. Any surprise?

The message we took to the polls did not resonate. Our base rewarded us in 2006 by staying home on Election Day. I know that fatigue with the Iraq War played a major role in our loss. So too did the preposterous media-driven discontent with the Republicans over Hurricane Katrina. If you remember, they blamed the very weather on Bush and refused to acknowledge how much better the Republican Gulf states handled the hurricane than New Orleans did.

All that said, if our core supporters had believed in what we were doing, we would not have lost thirty seats and the control of the House for the first time in twelve years. I have to give my constituents credit for knowing the positions I was taking. I received nearly ten thousand more votes than I did in the 2002 off-year election and won handily. Still, the loss of so many Republicans was devastating. In the days afterward, I was reluctant to talk to my colleagues in Congress, unsure at a glance of who had won and who had lost.

I had some sense of what was to come. After all, I had spent twelve years in the minority in the Missouri House, and I knew what it was like to always be playing defense. In Congress, however, the stakes were higher, namely America's future, not just the future of one of the fifty states. And it would only get worse, much worse, when new Speaker Nancy Pelosi got a president who thought the way she did.

# 10

# GOING TO WAR

**W**hen I asked for a slot on the Armed Services Committee, I presumed I would be working to improve a peacetime military. As a former US Army combat engineer, I thought I could contribute to the process. Besides, I believed that the most essential function of the federal government is to defend the country. By serving on this committee, I would be doing work that was clearly supported by the Constitution, and that mattered to me.

The Armed Services Committee was less partisan than many other committees, and as a result, useful things got done there. After September 11, 2001, our work took on a new urgency. In the years ahead, I would hear over and over again about "George Bush's illegal war," as though he had somehow taken the country in a direction it did not want to go and done so in disregard of the United States Constitution. That was nonsense. According to the Constitution, Congress "shall have Power . . . to declare War, grant Letters of Marque and Reprisal, and make Rules concerning Captures on Land and Water."

In this spirit, three days after the attacks of 9/11, the House and the Senate in a joint resolution passed an Authorization for Use of Military Force that enabled the president to use all "necessary and appropriate force" against those whom he determined "planned, authorized, committed or aided" the September 11 attacks, or who harbored said persons or groups.[1]

This resolution passed the Senate 98–0 and the House 420–1. This defense measure was as constitutionally sound a measure as Congress has ever passed. Truman launched the Korean War and Kennedy and Johnson the Vietnam War without anything nearly as solid, not even close. For the record, Barbara Lee of California was the only nay vote in Congress. The vote made this former Black Panther auxiliary member a hero of the antiwar movement, a movement that would pick up considerable Democratic support as it became politically expedient to oppose our war efforts.

I did not have any reservations about my vote. Almost no one did in either party. As I see it, the one essential role of government is to assure justice internally and externally. That includes protecting the nation from those who would deny us our civil liberties, as our enemies in this unconventional war surely would do if they could. The fact that we were not attacked by a nation state but by an entity that found safe harbor within several nation states complicated our response, but this was hardly unique in our nation's history.

During the terms of our first three American presidents, the Barbary pirates of North Africa attacked American shipping. These pirates came from a group of six Muslim city-states that believed it their religious duty to capture ships and cargo and to kill or sell the crews into slavery. We had no capacity to stop them, and so they extracted increasing tribute, one year topping 20 percent of federal revenues. In response, President Adams commissioned and built a US Navy, including the USS *Constitution*, affectionately known as "Old Ironsides." In his first year as president, 1801, Thomas Jefferson sent a squadron of US Navy ships to deal with these rogue states, but it was not until 1815 that commodores William Bainbridge and Stephen Decatur routed the enemy and ended all tribute payments by the United States. Lesson from history: at times we must use our military to remove a safe haven from which enemies are attacking us. To accomplish this, we must have a strong national defense. Another lesson: Americans have little patience for long, protracted wars.[2]

Our initial thrust into Afghanistan in 2001 would have made Thomas Jefferson proud. We adapted a modern strategy to a backward country. We put special-ops people on the ground, and not many of them, and they worked with the Afghan Northern Alliance. Together they effectively blocked communications and supply lines and threw the Taliban into disarray.

You would not have known how well this strategy was working from following the mainstream media. On October 31, 2001, the *New York Times* ran a front-page story headlined "A Military Quagmire Remembered: Afghanistan as Vietnam."[3] Although we were still enjoying something of a sabbatical from everyday bickering in Congress, President Bush's critics were always looking for an opening to undermine his leadership. Just weeks into the Afghan expedition, they were repeating the word "quagmire" as though we were replaying events in South Vietnam, the fall of which many Democrats actually enjoyed. "Are we quagmiring ourselves again?" the *Times'* Maureen Dowd asked hopefully.[4]

Yes, hopefully. People like Dowd, still burned by the closeness of the 2000 election, wanted Bush to fail. Disappointment came their way quickly. Kabul fell less than two weeks after the *New York Times* and others had decided Afghanistan was going to be another Vietnam. The fact that we are still there says much more about Barack Obama's indecisiveness, if not his downright indifference, than about the stunning effectiveness of the initial strategy.

On October 16, 2002, after much prodding by Democrats in Congress, Bush asked us for authorization to go to war in Iraq. There were some in the White House who argued that Congress had granted the president that authorization with the September 2001 vote authorizing the War on Terror, but I was pleased to see the White House come to Congress to authorize this new action. As a constitutionalist,

I believe that all significant military ventures, whether they are called "wars" or not, should get congressional approval.

The bill that came to the House was cosponsored by Speaker Denny Hastert and Minority Leader Dick Gephardt. Gephardt came from a neighboring district in Missouri. He was friendly enough, and in his ambition to become president, he seemed to have all the superficialities down pat, but I always wondered on talking with him: "Where is the real Dick Gephardt?" In this case, though, he did the right thing, especially given that most Democrats were planning to vote against authorization.

By the time this resolution came to Congress, the hard left in the Democratic Party had let it be known that they were opposed to any war, especially one that Republicans led. The House members who represented hard-core Democratic districts were more fearful of offending their base than they were of Saddam Hussein's WMDs (weapons of mass destruction). Some 126 of these Democrats voted against the bill, but 82 Democrats and 215 Republicans joined together to authorize the war with more than a 2 to 1 majority. Given what we and the UN knew then, it was exactly the right vote.

In the Senate, the majority of Democrats voted in favor of authorization. This included all those with presidential ambitions, including Hillary Clinton, John Kerry, Joe Biden, Chris Dodd, and John Edwards. Although Ted Kennedy voted against authorization, it was not because of some particular insight into Saddam Hussein's intentions. "We have known for many years that Saddam Hussein is seeking and developing weapons of mass destruction," said Kennedy just one month before the vote.

No, Kennedy opted to maintain his reputation as the godfather of the American left, weapons of mass destruction notwithstanding. John Kerry, already angling for the presidency during a period of heightened patriotism, was even more forceful. "[W]ithout question, we need to disarm Saddam Hussein. He is a brutal, murderous dictator, leading an oppressive regime," said Kerry in January 2003. "The threat of Saddam Hussein with weapons of mass destruction is real."[5]

On March 15, 2003, long-shot presidential candidate Howard Dean gave a speech in California that resonated throughout the Democratic back rooms of America. "What I want to know is what in the world so many Democrats are doing supporting the president's unilateral intervention in Iraq?" asked Dean.[6] He said this five days before the war started, a war he had already pegged as "the president's."

As to the "unilateral" bit, he might want to share that thought with the 179 British mothers whose sons died in Iraq or the mothers from the 23 other coalition countries whose children died in that same war.

I had a son in the war as well. On the most memorable of my fact-finding trips, I met up with Perry, then a US Marine first lieutenant and combat engineer, in the hottest of hot spots, Fallujah. In speaking to him and his colleagues, I got a different message than I did from the generals. What they needed most, a major with Perry told me, were up-armored HMMWVs (high mobility multiwheeled vehicles), commonly known as "Humvees."

Originally, the Humvee was designed to move personnel behind the battle lines. As such, the vehicle was made largely out of lightweight aluminum, which made it easier to transport by aircraft. It didn't have much armor and wasn't designed to have people shooting at it. In Iraq, however, it was pressed into service in contested areas, so there was a rush to reinforce them not only against weapons fire but also against the dreaded IEDs (improvised explosive devices). What I learned on this trip was that many units in heated combat zones were still using the old Humvees reinforced with metal plates that the Marines had bolted to the sides. The newly designed Humvees, called "up-armored," were made with thick steel armor and bulletproof windows. However, these armored vehicles were being stored in Kuwait, and those going into country were being distributed randomly across Iraq and not going where they were needed most.

To make the situation worse, the military leaders had a system for categorizing what level of armor was being used in battle but had changed what each category meant without notifying anyone in Congress. We were told that only a certain level of armored Humvees were allowed to leave the protection of the bases. What we didn't know was that this "acceptable" level now was changed to include a number of subcategories that included everything from a vehicle with cobbled together armor and no side windows to the new highly armored Humvees with bulletproof glass windows. The military had redefined the levels so that nearly every Humvee they had was the "acceptable" level. I was not too happy to learn of this linguistic stunt.

When I returned to Washington, I implored our stalwart Armed Services Committee chair, California's Duncan Hunter, to address the problem, and that he did. The Humvees were moved out of Kuwait and into the zones where they were needed most. I got my greatest reward a year or so later when visiting Perry, then back in the states at Camp Lejeune in North Carolina. One of his fellow Marines from a different unit told me how his newly up-armored Humvee had struck an IED. It totaled the Humvee, but he walked away from the incident unscathed. "Congressman Akin," he said, "thanks for saving my life." I scarcely deserved that kind of credit, but I surely appreciated the sentiment. It reminded me that a congressman can make a tangible difference.

Once we had gotten into the war and it had not ended cleanly in less than seven months like the Gulf War, congressional Democrats began to waver in their support or, worse, claim that they were somehow deceived into voting for the war. Their fallback position became something along the lines of, "I am against the war, but I support the troops." Those troops included my son Perry and his two younger brothers, Micah and Ezra, who had followed Perry to the Naval Academy and were now Marines.

I didn't buy the Democrats' slippery words for a minute. They wanted to appear patriotic while undermining the war effort.

In 2007, the Democrats had introduced a resolution to block the funding for the president's surge strategy. The surge was a necessary and ultimately successful corrective to prevent Iraq from falling into chaos. I took to the House floor and gave a speech illustrating the inconsistency of their efforts to defund the war while allegedly supporting the troops.

"So to say that we are going to support our troops but that we are not going to send them any reinforcements is on the face of it contradictory," I said. "Could you picture Davy Crockett at the Alamo looking at his BlackBerry, getting a message from Congress? 'Davy Crockett, we support you. The only thing is we are not going to send any troops.' I'm sure that would really be impressive to Davy Crockett."

In conclusion, I explained how Lulli and I had trained our children in patriotism. They learned that defending the rights enumerated in our Declaration was a solemn duty. I showed a picture of my sons as children in their little uniforms, having a flag-raising ceremony with their self-created "Marine's Club." I then cut to a picture of Perry with about twenty of his fellow Marines standing in front of a massive ordnance cache they had discovered in Fallujah. This was a strong close.

It was all very personal to me. I was still smarting from Sen. John Kerry's smug comment a few months earlier to an audience of college students, "If you make an effort to be smart, you can do well. If you don't, you get stuck in Iraq."[7] Perry was eleventh in his class at the Naval Academy. He did not get "stuck" in Iraq. Like his fellow Marines, he went there to serve his country. He knew the risks. In fact, twenty-four hours after my visit to Fallujah, Perry narrowly escaped being killed in a mortar attack. By God's grace, the 120-millimeter mortar round that landed twelve feet from him didn't detonate.

The Left didn't want to deal with reason, so, as they usually do, they ridiculed the speech I gave about the importance of funding our troops. Keith Olbermann named me "Worst Person in the World" because of my presentation.[8] As Jon Stewart of *The Daily Show* put it, "Actually, I have to think if Davy Crockett had received a message on his BlackBerry from anybody, it would have been very impressive." He and others took glee in pointing out that the

BlackBerry had not yet been invented. That, of course, was obvious, but leftists are so confident of their own superiority that they believe only they notice the obvious. What they lacked was the intellectual capacity or integrity to see the analogy of Crockett getting verbal "support" but no military help at the Alamo.

The media were quick to mock the BlackBerry reference, but it didn't end there. "It turns out that few people could picture the late Mr. Crockett with a BlackBerry in 1836," Ray Hartmann would write in a May 2010 *St. Louis* magazine article, "but even fewer seemed to understand Akin's sense of history or humor." Earlier in this article, Ray Hartmann ridiculed my prayer that we as a nation "don't make this fatal step pushing our nation into socialized medicine." Back then, opposing Obamacare was as funny as trying to save Iraq from falling into the hands of Al-Qaeda. Praying about either was particularly hysterical—testament, said Hartmann, to my "wing-nut theology."[9] I suspect that if Hartmann were hunkered down in a Fallujah foxhole, he would not find prayer quite so amusing.

In 2010, then Speaker Nancy Pelosi showed how little respect she had for national defense by sneaking a provision into the National Defense Authorization Bill (NDA) that would extend federal hate crime laws to include violence against gays, a law that didn't have any connection with the military and clearly did not belong. I did not want the provisioning of my kids and their colleagues to be held hostage for liberal experimentation, and I protested loudly. Bills should only have germane topics therein.

The Republican leadership in the House buckled in the face of Pelosi's underhanded move, a response not uncommon by the Republican leadership. I requested that Republican House leaders call a Republican caucus meeting, but they refused. To force a meeting, I had to get fifty signatures from my colleagues, and when minority leader John Boehner saw that I was about to succeed, he yielded. It was one of the most candid and spirited caucus meetings I would attend.

Pelosi had obviously leaned on Missouri's Ike Skelton, then

chairman of the Armed Services Committee, and he was none too pleased to see this sudden Republican resistance to a bill that had already passed the Senate and seemed a done deal in the House. If my conservative colleagues were beginning to talk of me as the conscience of the Republican House, Skelton had some less kind words. After I said on the floor that we Republicans "refuse to be blackmailed into voting for a piece of social agenda that has no place in this bill," Skelton said under his breath, but loud enough to be picked up by C-SPAN's cameras, "Stick it up your [bleep]."[10]

During the next several hours, a media brushfire swept the District. I refused to play the liberals' game of feigned outrage and refrained from stoking the flames. Our official response: "We were surprised by his statement—we felt it was out of character." In several radio interviews, with tongue firmly in cheek, I said we were "investigating whether a 'hate crime' had been committed."

In the next election, Republican Vicky Hartzler used Skelton's words to unseat him after seventeen terms in Congress. Skelton died while I was writing this book. We did not always see eye to eye, but we both saw the historic need for a strong national defense. Unfortunately, he represented a minority within the Democrat Party.

# 11

# THE AGE OF OBAMA

"**T**his campaign in the next couple of weeks is about one thing," I told the audience at a McCain rally outside St. Louis in 2008. "It's a referendum on socialism." Socialism? The media, of course, gasped. They had long ago convinced themselves that Obama was, in the words of *Politico*'s John Avlon, "a post-partisan centrist." Said Avlon, voicing the conventional wisdom in 2008, "He's been a bridge-builder all his life, first between black and white, and now between left and right."[1] Yeah, right.

Obama's liberalism was no secret. Just the previous year, the nonpartisan *National Journal* magazine rated Obama as "the most liberal senator." This was the same Obama whose mentor as a young man was Frank Marshall Davis, a card-carrying member of the Communist Party USA; the same Obama who felt comfortable "palling around" with terrorists like Bill Ayers and Bernardine Dohrn; the same Obama who flanked Hillary Clinton to the Left with his precocious opposition to the Iraq War; the same Obama who had recently shared his commitment to wealth redistribution with Joe "the Plumber" Wurzelbacher, "When you spread the wealth around, it's good for everybody." But other than Obama's Senate record and his hard left background, the media and our Republican elite assured us there was nothing to worry about.

The Beltway Republicans were naïve to a fault. David Brooks, the former *Weekly Standard* writer who moved to the *New York Times* in 2003, said of Obama, "I remember distinctly an image of—we were sitting on his couches, and I was looking at his pant leg and his perfectly creased pant, and I'm thinking, a) he's going to be president, and b) he'll be a very good president."[2] Perfectly creased pants? Was Brooks, I wondered, now writing a column on tailoring for the *Times'* Style section?

Former Reagan speechwriter Peggy Noonan has done much to promote the conservative cause, but in this case, she certainly misjudged Obama. In October 2008, she actually wrote of Obama, "He has within him the possibility to change the direction and tone of American foreign policy. . . . His victory would provide a fresh start in a nation in which a fresh start would come as a national relief."[3] A relief from what? Common sense? What were these people thinking? What were they drinking?

"I intellectually don't know how you cannot figure out Barack Obama—a liberal is a liberal," said Rush Limbaugh years later, in response to this continued dithering by the Beltway swells. "I know Obama, for the low-information crowd, could be whatever you wanted him to be, a blank canvas. But for crying out loud, we're not talking about low-information people here."[4] I had to agree with Rush, a fellow Show-Me Stater, on this one. Maybe there is something in the Missouri water that makes us born skeptics. If you're a leftist, you can't just say you're a centrist and expect us to buy it. In Missouri at least, you have to show us.

Although I backed John McCain in his futile effort to deny Obama the presidency, McCain never did strike me as a potential president. I had met him personally at the US Naval Academy in Annapolis when I was visiting my son. I respected his service to America, but he seemed old, brittle, and internally angry. During the primary season, he allowed the media to attack Bush with impunity.

When they were finished, there was nothing we could stand for. On domestic issues, McCain was all over the map. I could never trust where he would come down on a given issue. Needless to say, McCain was not my favorite candidate in the 2008 Republican primaries.

I had met with Romney several times. He said the right things and seemed hungry. He had strong business and economic credentials, but his inconsistent record on the life issue was a concern, as was the Massachusetts state health care reform he had championed. In 2012, Romney's chief adviser confirmed my misgivings when he described Romney's general election strategy as follows, "It's almost like an Etch-A-Sketch. You can kind of shake it up and restart all over again."[5]

In 2012, I had great respect for Newt Gingrich and Michele Bachmann, whom I had gotten to know over a period of years. I also, from a distance, liked Mike Huckabee, the former Arkansas governor. Some conservatives who cared most about economic issues were vocally against him, but I deeply respected his stand on social issues, and he respected mine. He was still my favorite. Later, I got to know Mike better by hosting a big reception for him at the Capitol Hill Club. We had more than seventy members of Congress attend. It was a good event.

This brings me to a point that the media refuse to understand. Most social conservatives of my acquaintance are more consistent champions of free enterprises and free markets than many self-identified economic conservatives or libertarians. What is more, we see the essential connection between the two strains of conservative thought. The loss of 55 million citizens killed through abortion has had economic repercussions, such as reduced funding for Social Security and workforce shortages. Then too, when the moral order begins to fray, the whole social fabric can unravel. There is not much distance between "Thou shalt not kill" and "Thou shalt not steal" (Exodus 20:13, 15). A 50 percent divorce rate, another social issue, carries a heavy federal price tag in dependency. The societal price tag for unwed motherhood is even greater.

As the 2008 campaign wound down, it became clear that the

election was less about issues than about personality. The media were caught in a collective swoon over Obama and were imposing their newfound passion on their audiences. McCain did hold Missouri, and I received more votes in my congressional election than I ever had before, and hugely more than McCain. However, not every state had voters as smart as Missouri. Obama captured the presidency. That was going to hurt.

As painful as Obama's victory was, those of us who did not vote for him saw a glimmer of hope in his election. We all believed that having a partially African American president in the White House would help lessen the nation's racial divide. Unfortunately, by yelling, "Racism!" every time anyone criticized the president's policies, Obama's fellow Democrats and their allies in the media have only aggravated racial tensions. I am not just speculating. In January 2009, according to a poll taken by NBC News and the *Wall Street Journal,* 79 percent of whites and 63 percent of blacks held a favorable view of race relations in America. By July 2013, those figures had fallen to 52 percent among whites and 38 percent among blacks.[6] This was the opposite of what was supposed to happen.

Disappointment came quickly on another front as well. On January 22, 2009, a cool and bright Thursday two days after the inauguration, more than three hundred thousand people from all over America descended on Washington for the annual March for Life. Although it would be more comfortable and convenient to stage the march in the middle of April, as the Earth Day people do, the March for Life organizers stick to January 22 because that date resonates in American history. It was the day in 1973 when a progressive Supreme Court tossed out every state abortion law in the country and imposed its will on the people of America—*Roe v. Wade.*

In their alleged wisdom, the justices found the right to an abortion hidden deep in the penumbra of the due process clause of the Fourteenth Amendment. This was the most consequential US Supreme Court overreach since the Dred Scott decision of 1857, when the justices ruled that a person of African descent could not claim citizenship in the United States—in other words, once a slave, always a slave. What the two decisions had in common was that each was decided by a seven-to-two majority, and each denied personhood to a large class of vulnerable humanity.

I spoke briefly to the marchers as I did every year I was in Congress. I felt it was important for me to be in the march to address and encourage them. These people were dedicated. They were willing to ride a bus across the country, often getting their sleep in their bus seats. Seeing such dedication reminded me of the spirit that motivated George Washington's troops to the Delaware. They endured hardships because their cause was just. I am thankful for the dedication these pro-life marchers have for a just cause. What wonderful, fellow American compatriots! Afterward, as usual, we held a reception for the marchers in the lobby of the Cannon Building, complete with coffee, hot chocolate, cookies, and other finger foods—this, for some, was their only non-backpacked meal on their three-day bus journey.

The election of Obama had galvanized the pro-life movement. More people showed up for this march than any in history. Always optimistic, the marchers hoped they just might get the attention of the media and win the heart of the new president. Unfortunately, they did neither. The media gave as much attention to a handful of pro-abortion protestors as they did to the three hundred thousand or so marchers, and the president rewarded the marchers' efforts with a slap in the face. The very next day he issued an executive order that repealed existing rules and reauthorized federal money to go to international organizations that promote or provide abortions overseas. Any illusion I might have had about Obama's centralism was dispelled that sad January day.

The issue of life is the most fundamental issue in defining who and what our nation is. Any Republican leader who tells you that we should shy away from this issue should be handed an enrollment form for the Democratic Party. As Obama quickly proved, the Democratic Party is where abortion supporters belong. By day three of his administration, I felt that everything we'd struggled for was going to be reversed.

For twelve years I had labored in the minority in the Missouri House, so I was not unfamiliar with having to play defense, but these next two years would be the most frustrating of my legislative career. Our constituents wanted us to do something, but there was very little we could do because the Democrats had control of both Houses of Congress, the presidency, and, of course, the media. I could have lit my hair on fire, and it would have changed nothing.

For those Republicans who were still wondering whether Obama was a centrist, he was doing everything in his power to sober them up. In 2009, he proposed a triumvirate of bad ideas, a massive expansion of government power in three major sectors of the American economy: energy, finance, and, of course, health care. On the energy front, the administration led with the American Clean Energy and Security Act of 2009 (ACES).

This was a remarkably stupid bill based on an entirely dubious premise, namely, that man was causing the earth to overheat to dangerous levels. To solve that imagined problem, ACES promised one of those notoriously convoluted cap-and-trade systems. The government would set a limit (cap) on the greenhouse gasses produced nationally, and companies would then buy or sell permits to emit these gases. As the Heritage Foundation pointed out, even if the alarmist science was valid, this plan would reduce global temperature by no more than two-tenths of a degree by the end of the century.[7]

If this energy marketplace sounds something like the health care exchanges under Obamacare, there is a reason why. In each case, the government tried to create a false scarcity and to oversee the disbursement of goods, a first step toward government ownership. So important was the June 2009 vote for the Democrats that they roused Patrick Kennedy out of rehab and apparently got a designated driver to bring him to the House floor for the vote.

Even sober, young Mr. Kennedy was not one of the Democrats we managed to win over. These forty-four Dems would have been enough to defeat the legislation, but eight blue-state Republicans voted for the bill, allowing it to pass narrowly. After the vote, the media could not sing Obama's praises loudly enough, calling the vote "historic" and the passage a "triumph" for the president. If our liberal Republican friends celebrated the victory, I wasn't invited to the party.

As this legislation moved through the House, we were able to educate not just the citizens, not just our fellow legislators, but in this case the corporate leaders most directly affected by this government manipulation. They were listening. As they understood, senators are more dependent on big business for financial support than are House members. Senate majority leader Harry Reid quickly discovered he did not have enough votes to bring the legislation to the floor, and there it died a quiet death. Indifferent to constitutional niceties, President Obama promised to advance the cause of climate change—whatever that means—through regulatory changes and executive orders. Unfortunately, he has been as good as his word.

The Democrats had more success on the financial front. In July 2010, President Obama signed into law the Wall Street Reform and Consumer Protection Act of 2009, a monstrosity of a bill so complex and contradictory that it defies rational explanation. The bill is more commonly known as Dodd-Frank after its coauthors, Rep. Barney Frank of Massachusetts and Sen. Chris Dodd of Connecticut. Yes, this was the same Chris Dodd that was a VIP customer of Countrywide Financial, the lending operation at the heart of the housing market collapse. And yes, this was the same Barney Frank who in 2005 scolded those of us who worried about an impending housing crash.

"You are not going to see the collapse that you see when people talk about a bubble," Frank told us. "So those on our committee in particular are going to continue to push for homeownership."[8] Push he did, and the bubble did indeed burst. Dodd and Frank both kept their jobs. I have always tried to focus my critiques not on people but on bad ideas. On this point, Barney Frank tested my resolve.

Obama's most important piece of legislation, of course, was the so-called Patient Protection and Affordable Care Act, an epic piece of nonsense that wasn't affordable and protected no patients, but the administration deceived America into thinking it would do both. I could write a book on just how disastrous this whole thing has been, but I am sure lots of people have beaten me to it already. It was the worst possible bill I had ever seen. Because this bill came up for a vote in March 2010, when Democrats controlled both chambers and the presidency, several of my conservative congressional friends and I decided to use Ronald Reagan's tactics and take our case directly to the public. At literally every opportunity, we educated anyone who would listen on the dangers of Obamacare. So started a many-month heroic uphill battle against socialized medicine. Leading the charge were a dozen articulate Republican Congressmen who are doctors and a number of us who were leaders of the newly created Tea Party Caucus.

One example of my efforts along these lines was an "anti-Obamacare" rally that we staged at the St. Charles convention center when Obama was visiting the St. Louis area. The rally featured live appearances by many local Republicans, including the lieutenant governor, and I teleconferenced in from Washington, DC. Wednesday morning was not an ideal time to attract the participants we needed to upstage Obama's event, but in addition to our loyal congressional base, we were able to tap into the energy of the most significant grassroots movement in recent American history, the Tea Party. We hoped for five hundred people. Nearly twenty-five hundred showed up.

Given the Tea Party's success, the Democrats accused the movement of being pure "Astroturf," meaning artificially grown. This is where you incentivize people to show up. The Democrats know about Astroturf. Their "activists" almost inevitably show up at protests in buses, often lured by the thought of free pizza or an outright payday. But our rally wasn't like this. Tea Party people take their cars or, just as likely, their trucks. No one tells them to go anywhere. No one gives them anything when they get there.

Contrary to Democratic fantasies, Tea Partiers show up on their own volition and usually only when faced with some serious offense to their wallets or the Constitution. Obamacare offended both. Invariably, Tea Partiers clean up after themselves much better than the allegedly "green" Democrats. These people are the salt of the earth and the heart and soul of the Republican Party and America.

The Tea Party belies the nonsense that Republicans are the party of the rich. Most of America's wealthiest counties are Democratic. The richest, Loudon County, Virginia, gave Obama 52 percent of its vote in 2012. The second richest, Fairfax County, Virginia, voted 59 percent for Obama. And if you think this is just a Beltway fallout factor, consider California's wealthiest county, Marin. There, Obama got 74 percent of the vote. He got more than 70 percent in nearby Sonoma and San Mateo counties and more than 60 percent in Napa. The motto "Show-Me State" still has resonance. People from Marin County in California may be wealthier than those in St. Louis County, Missouri, but their liberal voting patterns certainly don't show a wealth of common sense. So, contrary to media pitch, the wealthiest counties actually vote Democratic.

On Easter Sunday at 11 a.m., about two dozen of us went to the chapel. On our knees, individually taking turns leading the prayers, we appealed to the Lord for deliverance. There was hardly a dry eye in the chapel. After we finished praying, I led our little band of resisters in a spontaneous rendition of "Amazing Grace." Later that morning, Obamacare came to the floor for a vote. Our efforts had delayed the bill for many months, but it passed, and we were heartsick for our country. As history will remind our descendants, not a single Republican in either the House or the Senate voted for Obamacare, one of the most transformative and totally corrupt pieces of legislation in American history.

Although that afternoon we felt beaten, we came to realize that our mighty effort had succeeded in warning the American public. As public opinion polls have shown from that day forward, most Americans wanted nothing to do with Obamacare.

I believe this uphill, one-sided battle was one of the greatest struggles in which my colleagues and I have ever participated.

Together, we shared an unusual harmony, common purpose, and sense of team effort. There were some real heroes in that room, and to this day, I feel a deep affection for my fellow comrades in arms. I believe God heard our fervent prayers. Was anyone else listening? You be the judge. Spurred by the Tea Party, Republican voters flooded the polls in 2010 and allowed us to pick up sixty-three seats in the House and at least partly restrain Obama's Constitution-wrecking for at least the next four years.

# 12

# RUNNING FOR THE SENATE: 2011

**W**hen I headed back to Washington for the 2011 session, the world looked much more promising than it had a year earlier. Republicans now controlled the House. While it is unlikely that we would be able to get any significant legislation passed through the Democratic Senate or approved by the White House, we could and would play some serious defense. It was nice to be relevant once again.

Our first meeting after the election was a very serious occasion. There were no high-fives or joking around. We felt that by giving us the majority in the House, the public had entrusted us with a solemn responsibility. Many of us believed that we were all that stood in the way of the federal takeover of America. As a member of the House Budget Committee, one of my first priorities was to use the momentum of the Republican takeover to start fixing the federal budget system.

Our Constitution originally established the legislative branch as the most powerful. It was the one most accountable to the people and therefore was given the responsibility of the public's purse. Through the years, the legislature has been losing its power because the executive branch largely controls the budget. Conservatives had to change existing rules if progress was to be made. To shake things up, I proposed that the Republicans in the House create a committee to redesign the budget system. As an aside, the "earmark" debate was a distraction that affected about 1 percent of the budget. The real deal was an overhaul of the budget system.

I offered my proposal at a major Republican congressional organizational meeting in January 2011. After I explained the proposal, Speaker Boehner rose and said that he agreed with everything I had laid out. However, he asked me to withdraw my amendment because he wanted to handle the problem in his own way. Lacking the votes to challenge him, I took Boehner at his word. I shouldn't have. As far as I know, nothing has been done since. That's the way Washington rolls.

I might note that within the Republican Congress there were several changes taking place at this time. Many of the new Republicans who were part of the Tea Party class were soft on national defense. In the past, every fiscal conservative I knew was pro-defense. Also, I started to see tension build between conservatives and pragmatists under Boehner's leadership.

Some months later, at the Missouri State Lincoln Days in Springfield, something unexpected occurred. John and Merre Putnam, two dear friends from many years ago, set up a booth at the conference and sent out an e-mail resolution drafting me to run for the US Senate. John is the many times grand-nephew of *the* Israel Putnam, the battle commander at Bunker Hill who famously said, "Don't shoot until you see the whites of their eyes."

To that point, I had not contemplated running, at least not seriously. In 2006, Claire McCaskill had beaten Jim Talent for a Senate seat that Talent had held for four years after winning a special election in 2002. Although 2006 was a banner year for Democrats, McCaskill barely beat Talent and got less than 50 percent of the vote. I figured—everyone did—that Talent would want another shot at that seat, and I had no intention of challenging him in the primary. He had run statewide several times before. I never had. Name identification and experience are critical in a statewide race.

Talent had to have been tempted. McCaskill had left herself vulnerable on several fronts. For one, she supported Barack Obama and his pet legislation, Obamacare. She not only voted for the individual mandate amendment, but she also traveled the state, defending the legislation at a series of often-hostile town hall–style meetings. Her message was apparently not well received. In August 2010, in the nation's first plebiscite on the Obamacare mandate, a resounding 71 percent of Missourians voted to nullify it. This vote got a good deal of national attention and alerted McCaskill that she would have a battle on hand come 2012.

McCaskill's reelection chances were further jeopardized in 2011 when Missouri citizens learned that she had been billing the public for private travel on her husband's eight-seat, twin-engine airplane. In reviewing the "oversight"—so the story went—McCaskill discovered that she had not paid nearly three hundred thousand dollars in personal property taxes on the aircraft.[1] These shenanigans made national news, rare for a Democrat, and a sign of their seriousness.

For all her flaws, McCaskill had one major advantage over any Republican candidate: the full-throated support of the state's major media. She would have more than a year to recover from the airplane fiasco, and the impending Obamacare disaster would not yet have played out in public. Still, to compensate for her missteps, she and her media allies would have to pin something horrible on her Republican challenger. I suppose I should have seen that coming.

Jim Talent did not wait long to throw the race wide open. On January 27, 2011, he announced he would *not* be running. By that time, former Missouri treasurer Sarah Steelman had announced she would be running. Although attractive and sincere, Steelman had failed in her attempt to win the Republican nomination for governor a few years prior. Everyone suspected that she would have competition for the nomination, but even I was uncertain that this competition would include me.

I have always paid very close attention to my then ninety-year-old father. When he suggested that I should enter the race, I explained it would be a mammoth undertaking and cost as much as $15 or $20 million. He told me that someone had to step up. Obama and McCaskill could not be allowed free reign. He concluded by asking, "If you don't do it, who will?" When I asked around, it was becoming obvious that none of the other Republican Members of Congress was willing to give up a safe House seat for a risky run against a wily incumbent. So if not me, who?

So why would I give up a safe House seat where I knew and respected my constituents and where I had been elected with overwhelming majorities? Why would I volunteer to spend two arduous years traveling all over the state, making endless calls asking for money—never my favorite activity? The answers were not the obvious ones.

From the beginning, I had taught my children that the blessings of life, liberty, and the pursuit of happiness came from our Creator. I taught them that generations of Americans had risked or given their lives to protect these blessings. And more to the point, I taught them that these blessings were theirs to defend as well. This was a responsibility they accepted. Three of the boys attended the US Naval Academy in Annapolis, and upon graduation, all three joined the US Marines. I could not have been more pleased, even though the pleasure was mixed with anxiety. As a Marine platoon commander, Perry experienced three very close calls in Fallujah in 2005. I worried about him every day.

But I worried about our country as well. Sad to say, I had no doubt that our own federal government represented a clear and present danger. America, whether she knew it or not, was in jeopardy. If I won the Senate seat, I would have the opportunity to do something about that threat to America from a position of real authority—one out of a hundred instead of one out of 435 votes. I had the potential to win, I knew, and I had the requisite experience gained through the school of legislative hard knocks to succeed. As

I saw it, it was my turn, like my sons and many sons before me, to put everything on the line for freedom's cause. The decision was a sober one. I was all in, and I wasn't turning back. Win or lose, I had a sense of peace, but never for a second did I think that either the primary or the general race would be easy sledding.

On May 17, 2011, at the Drury Inn in Creve Coeur, before a room packed with media, I announced my intention to run for the US Senate. Joining me on the small stage were Lulli, my son Wynn, and our two daughters Hannah and Abigail. The speech I gave was short, fewer than five minutes, and low-key. This was not the time for podium pounding. As I explained, America had to choose between two different futures: the Democratic future of big government and reckless spending, or a conservative future characterized by limited government and freedom. I also highlighted some of my difficult but principled votes, including a vote against President Bush's very first piece of legislation, No Child Left Behind; every bailout, including the Troubled Asset Relief Program (TARP) that Bush signed into law in October 2008; and Obama's infamous stimulus bill.

As to whether I was too conservative, I explained that given the current direction of the White House, conservative was the medicine that America needed. I rooted my conservatism in the wisdom of America's founding and even offered an obscure quote from the Declaration of Independence that seemed particularly apt in 2012: "He has erected a multitude of new offices by a self-assumed power, and sent hither swarms of officers to harass our people and eat out their substance." The "he" in question was, of course, King George III, but to many in the audience, it sounded a lot like King Barack I. In closing, I reiterated that my candidacy provided Missouri with a choice to pursue the course of limited government and freedom. The ovation I received was heartfelt and a little embarrassing in its enthusiasm. I loved these people, and I owed them my best.

In the Q & A that followed, no one in the media asked questions about the social issues. In 2012, we all knew that the battleground was going to be over economics with the question of health care front and center. I did not hesitate to call Obamacare "socialized medicine." I had no intention of speaking in euphemisms, and the media caught on to that quickly.

As to my positioning strategy against McCaskill, it was pretty straightforward. I was a conservative, but McCaskill was not the "moderate" she pretended to be. She voted with Obama 98 percent of the time and continued to support Obamacare even after Missourians resoundingly rejected it. I would just let it be known that our political philosophies were altogether opposite. McCaskill's liberal ideology aligned her with groups like Emily's List, which was her largest donor. McCaskill had amassed a significant war chest of $10 million from groups supporting abortion and other liberal causes.

From a political perspective, the reporter who asked me the last question touched on the topic that was most immediately relevant. The reporter asked me about the candidacy of Missouri businessman John Brunner. Brunner worked for a business his grandfather had started, much as I did early in my career, and John Brunner had served as CEO for thirty years. In 2006, he sold the company to a private equity firm for a healthy chunk of change, and in 2009, he resigned from its management. In 2012, Brunner was looking for a challenge, and he had time and money enough to make his voice heard. He also began hiring many of the state's more seasoned political operatives. Brunner was to become the wild card in the race.

I had known John's father well. He was a patriot and a regular contributor to my campaigns, as was John. While I knew that John Brunner supported conservative causes, his experience was in business and not in government. It takes a great deal of study and experience to apply the principles of good government and to understand the myriad issues confronting our nation. Public service in Congress is as much a discipline as other professions are. Would you go to a heart surgeon who had never done a bypass? Would you buy the stock of a company whose CEO had never run even a small business? Would you take your Ford to a mechanic who had never worked on cars?

Brunner waited until October 2011 to make his formal announcement—at a warehouse. "I know pundits and elitists will say this guy doesn't have any experience or qualifications as a politician," he said to those gathered. He then paused before adding his punch line, "Precisely."[2] With this the crowd laughed and applauded. "I'll match my experience as a manufacturer and a job creator against a career politician's resume of borrowing and spending anytime, anywhere," he continued.[3] Brunner would turn one of his biggest weaknesses into an advantage, but there were dangers. In dozens of Lincoln Day meetings, I would counter, "A proven record under fire beats talk and promises anytime."

Campaigns can be thought of as resting on three legs, like a stool: money, message, and grass roots. Though quarter after quarter I consistently out-fund-raised my opponents, I could not win a media slugfest with a man like Brunner who could spend millions of his own money. We would have to win on message and grass roots—our specialties. What surprised me, what surprised everyone, was that Brunner put ads up on TV and radio a month after announcing and stayed on the air for the entire race. He planned to go all in to win the seat, and that got some people's attention.

There were few Republicans in Congress who had a better record on economic issues than I did. I thought the conservative groups would endorse me without a second thought, but that wasn't the case.

The Club for Growth is an organization focused on cutting taxes and other economic issues, and it gave me a 92 percent lifetime rating. That put me easily in the top 10 percent of Congressional members. Ron Paul, for instance, had an 88 percent rating; Paul Ryan, 86 percent; John Boehner, 83; Eric Cantor, 79. The Club for Growth PAC should have endorsed me without a second thought. But they endorsed Brunner.

Club for Growth president Chris Chocola conceded that I "score highly" on economic issues, but he attacked my defense of earmarks.[4] "Score highly"? Only a handful of Republicans scored better, and none of those was in leadership. I also had a more conservative record than Chris himself did when he was a congressman.

The US Chamber chose to back Brunner as well. So did Freedom-Works, a libertarian, economic-oriented organization founded by David Koch. These organizations overlooked my A+ rating from the American Conservative Union, the top conservative ratings I received from the *National Journal,* twelve successive years of receiving the Chamber's "Spirit of Enterprise" award, and my "Taxpayer Hero" designation from Citizens Against Government Waste.

To Washington insiders, who are mostly preoccupied with picking winners and losers, Brunner's thick wallet trumped my twelve-year conservative record earned in the trenches under fire. Strange and inconsistent as this may seem, it is politics. Losing these important endorsements hurt because it meant losing hundreds of thousands of dollars in donations down the road, but as I said, I was running to win, and I wasn't turning back.

I thought of the great patriot heroes of the Bible and of America's Founders and saw a pattern in their efforts. They all strove to accomplish something that most thought impossible or hopeless, but they trusted God and gave it their all. I'm sure the friends of Shadrach, Meshach, and Abednego thought they were nuts, getting thrown into the fiery furnace. I suspect the Tory neighbors of our farmer forefathers thought them daft for taking on the biggest military power in the world.

My task was not nearly as daunting as that of these great heroes, but the pattern was much the same. I sensed God loved faith-filled followers who trust Him and try to do the difficult but right thing, regardless of the personal costs or results. The victory comes not on Election Day necessarily, but on the day that we conquer our fears and pursue the just cause. As Abigail Adams, wife of our second president, and mother of our fourth president, wrote, "A patriot without religion in my estimation is as great a paradox as an honest man without fear of God."

# 13

# RUNNING FOR THE SENATE: 2012

Sons are a heritage from the LORD, children a reward from him.
Like arrows in the hands of a warrior are sons born in one's youth.
Blessed is the man whose quiver is full of them. They will not be
put to shame when they contend with their enemies in the gate.
—Psalm 127:3–5 NIV

A s we rolled through the fourth quarter of 2011—actually, "stumbled through" is probably a more accurate term—it was becoming clear that we had an organizational problem on our hands. No one on our staff had either the experience or the talent to manage a statewide campaign. My staff people knew their own limitations in this regard, and a few were wilting under the pressure of trying to be something they were not.

I had been keeping an eye out for a good campaign manager, but no one I tried worked out. So, I did what I often did throughout the campaign—asked God for help, asked everyone in my family and close friends to pray, and then trusted Him to provide. He did.

Of all the people I knew and trusted, only one had the skill to do the job. I am speaking here of my son Perry.

Perry had acquired his skill under fire, literally, as a Marine pla-toon commander in Iraq and then as a battalion operations officer responsible for hundreds of personnel. After five-plus years in the Marines, he had gotten his MBA from the University of Chicago, graduating very near the top of his class, as he had from the US Naval Academy. I can't express how I felt the Sunday afternoon when I got the call from Perry and Amanda. They told me Perry would be willing to serve as campaign manager, at no pay, if I would have him.

I wanted him so badly I could taste it, but at first I felt his offer was too generous. How could I ask someone to give up a six-figure salary and move a family to another state to manage a campaign for a candidate few thought capable of winning? My risk-taking had gotten me into the race, but this was too much of a sacrifice to ask of a young family. Now, Perry was volunteering. He would not have made that expensive decision if he did not understand our country's dire need and did not believe in what we stood for.

There were, of course, some complications. For one, Perry had just assumed a new role in the sales and marketing group at John Deere in Moline and would have to take a leave of absence. For another, he had never managed a political campaign. For a third, he and his wife, Amanda, had five children, the oldest of whom was seven. For a fourth, he would not be able to accept a salary. For a fifth, he would have to move the family to St. Louis. And finally, he would have to make the move immediately.

Given who they are as a couple, Perry and Amanda approached the decision to manage the campaign by praying over it. Then, being the engineer he is, Perry evaluated the pluses and minuses of the decision. At the top of the plus list was the knowledge that I needed him. No outsider could hope to know how Lulli and I thought and what we valued better than one of our children. As our son, too, Perry would also be able to speak to me more openly and honestly than a paid adviser would dare.

Once he had made up his mind, Perry approached his bosses at John Deere to request a leave of absence. As a company, John Deere emphasizes the traits of integrity and commitment in everything one does. It was clear to Perry's bosses that it was these core traits that influenced his decision to help his father. They obviously respected Perry enough to grant him a ten-month leave of absence, a decision Perry recognized as gracious and affirming. With that problem solved, Perry and Amanda rented a truck, loaded it themselves, and moved their five little ones to a rental unit in the St. Louis area.

Perry's decision requires a word of explanation because not many children in this culture would make such a sacrifice. The chain of events goes back to one of the three most important decisions in my life, the education of my children. Over the years, my decision about how to educate my children has allowed me to become a truly "rich" man. The loving, healthy relations and family I enjoy is a gift from God that cannot be purchased. Our decision about education was very important.

Before we were married, Lulli and I agreed that she would leave her good job in IBM and stay home to raise our children and that I would support the family. In 1983, Lulli wanted to take our first son, Wynn, out of a Christian school and home-educate him. Although skeptical, I encouraged her to try. Boy, was I surprised. In four months Wynn's test scores had improved dramatically, but more importantly, so had his joy for life. We never went back. Around this time, thousands of parents all over America were making the same decision based in no small part on the belief that God was calling them to do so.

Through the years, Lulli and I came to realize that there are three basic questions regarding education. First, what do you teach? Second, how do you teach? And third, who does the teaching? We decided that the "what" began with the Bible. As to the "how," we were convinced that Jesus' example of apostleship/apprenticeship beat the homogenous-age classroom. This allows the students to look to an older sibling or adult for an example instead of someone their own age. Lastly, the "who," we believed, should be those with the primary responsibility to educate: namely, the parents.

We home educated our six kids until about age sixteen, or rather, until they went full time to college. By this point in our kids' lives they had a firm foundation of literature, mathematics, and grammar along with the courage to stand for what is right. In their midteens, when they were ready, we put the children in local college classes that would count for both high school and college credit. This also built critical time-management skills.

Like most of the early generation of home-educating parents, Lulli and I believed in the principle that parents are the primary educators. Ask any educator today, "What is the most important factor in good educational results?" They will almost always tell you that it is a parent's involvement. For most of us early home educators, we believed that this involvement should take the form of the parents being the primary educator. To many it was a conviction. For some this conviction came with the cost of going to jail or having their children taken away by the state. We believed it was our duty to educate our own children, and we would not delegate that responsibility to the state.

Home educating was also a preference that avoided some common classroom problems. It allowed each child to learn in each area at his or her own speed. This avoided the twin problems that many pupils find in a classroom: being left behind or not being challenged. If the class learns more quickly than you, you get left behind and soon believe that "you aren't good at school." Pupils with this mind-set become adults who don't learn new things necessary for their careers because "they aren't good at school." Conversely, if you learn more quickly than the class, you can become bored and dislike learning because it doesn't challenge you. Pupils with this experience can stop pushing themselves, dislike school, and never reach their potential. When a child is taught at home, the pace of material is matched to the child's own speed and keeps learning fun. Our kids, like many others we know, developed a mind-set that makes them learners for life.

Another side effect of home educating is that it is incredibly time and resource efficient, which makes for happier and better-rounded students. You don't have to take attendance. There isn't a fifteen-minute break to get to your next classroom. The teacher focuses on exactly the part the student doesn't understand. All these things save time. Then with the extra time, students can develop interests and hobbies, which make them better-rounded. Home educating is also efficient economically, which is probably one reason that home-educating families have many children.

There are dangers in a traditional school that go beyond education, one of them being the peer dependency generated in a classroom with peers all the same age. When children are dependent on peers for their affirmation, it limits their spontaneity and critical thinking. It also builds insecurity. Adults today are still haunted by stereotypes that go back to the old high school years and even to junior high years. In a homogenous-age classroom, kids tend to submit to politically correct ideas and rarely dare to challenge the status quo. In contrast, home-educated kids' primary interaction is with adults. What is cool is what adults say is cool. Funny, we even have an expression in English: "Grow up!" One side effect for us was six children and no teenage rebellion. They just grew up.

Above all else, home educating is about much more than education. It is about the delightful, rich, loving relationships within a close family. The special love and harmony are something money can't buy. It is this blessing that makes me a rich man. In addition, our family once again was to become a campaign asset.

I have included this material because of the generally low educational performance of America's government schools and, more importantly, as a suggestion for conservatives and patriots who are faced with the problem of the liberal control of education in general.

The day he arrived in St. Louis, Perry learned that he was expected to attend Morton Blackwell's weeklong premier campaign management school in Washington, DC, the very next morning. We hated to spring this on him, but we had just learned about it ourselves. It was too good an opportunity to pass up. I have never seen anyone work so hard and so well as Perry. Having led teams into combat in Fallujah, he did not feel that what he was doing was extraordinary, but I did. Perry had the right combination of people skills and management savvy to cut our expenses in half from the fourth quarter 2011 to the first quarter 2012 and build morale at the same time. That was no easy trick.

Within two months, Perry felt sufficiently comfortable with the nature of the campaign to serve as my proxy at events I could not attend since Congress was still in session. The first day Perry spoke on my behalf, he spoke to several hundred people at a gathering in St. Louis County. John Brunner took his turn first and attempted, as he often did, to paint me as a career politician, not a fresh entrepreneurial voice like him. As typical too, Brunner avoided specifics. He knew that he could frustrate the McCaskill people, Steelman, and me as well, if he gave us nothing to run against.

When Perry took his turn, he decided that he would not try to *be* me, but rather speak from his own experience. He liked telling stories. One story struck him as particularly on message. It took place back in Fallujah when he was stationed there in 2005. Some of the junior Marines under his command were green, and most had the good sense to be humble about it. One did not. This Marine liked to brag about how tough he was and how bad he wanted to face the enemy—that is, until he actually faced the enemy.

During the first real nighttime firefight, that junior Marine, a PFC, went missing. After looking everywhere, Perry's Marines found him under a truck, curled up in the fetal position. It was one thing to talk tough before you've been tested, Perry told the audience. It is another thing to stand your ground under fire. "When the president is calling you, demanding your vote for Medicare Part D," said Perry, "is when your mettle is tested. Only one Missouri candidate for US Senate has passed that test," Perry explained, "and it wasn't John Brunner." Brunner got the message. Going forward, I suspect, he was relieved when he only had to face me.

Perry always had my back. So did Wynn, Ezra, Micah, Hannah,

Abigail, and Lulli, especially Lulli. That's what family is for. As the Bible says, "They will not be put to shame when they contend with their enemies at the gate" (Psalm 127:5 NIV). God answers prayers in amazing ways. As it turned out, I had been training my campaign manager for more than twenty years!

# 14

# THE DANGEROUS
# CAMPAIGN TRAIL

The campaign trail gives candidates plenty of opportunities to practice honing their message. In Missouri, typically in February and March, county Republican organizations stage a gathering in honor of our party's first president, Abraham Lincoln. We call them "Lincoln Days." Attendees start with a little socializing, move to dinner, and then listen to a seemingly endless string of candidates tout their virtues for positions ranging from county clerk to US senator. Lincoln Days—sometimes expanded to Lincoln–Reagan Days—are the bread and butter of statewide Republican candidates.

In the early months of 2012, I attended a lot of Lincoln Days, as many as four in one night. I really enjoyed traveling the state, even in winter, even on the back roads, even in an Enterprise rental car. Lincoln Days and the grassroots party apparatus can be very helpful to the party overall. Among other things, these events allow regular citizens to personally see and meet the candidates. For those who attend, it requires patience to hear from as many as twenty politicians. For the candidates, it is tough to drive sometimes three or four hours to give just a two-minute speech. For those who, year after year, volunteer to set up and run the events, hats off!

The bottom-up system of local politics helps to preserve freedom. While the candidate may not think that a two-minute speech is enough time, people can often make a pretty accurate character snapshot in a meet and greet and from a short speech. As a result, local Republican voters frequently elect what party bosses consider "the wrong candidate" in the primary. They elect the conservative one. National party bosses want to reduce the influence of the local side of politics so they can pick "the correct candidate," namely, the wealthiest, the more "pragmatic" one—one more easily manipulated by the powers that be.

This is a very dangerous trend in Republican politics. It was particularly obvious in the US Senate Republican primaries in 2010 when Senate insiders like John Cornyn supported Charlie Crist over Marco Rubio in Florida and Trey Grayson over Rand Paul in Tennessee. The insiders want the power to pick their own liberal candidates. Yes, "liberal." Crist rewarded party bosses by running as a spoiler in the 2010 Senate race, endorsing Barack Obama, speaking at the 2012 Democratic National Convention, and then actually turning Democrat.

Because of the tremendous cost to run a campaign today, a candidate for federal office cannot be viable unless he or she is wealthy; he or she has built up a base of supporters who will fund the race; or he or she is well known for some other activity, such as sports, motion pictures, or media.

If moderates like Karl Rove are trusted with vast sums to support the "right" (more liberal) candidate in primaries, it will basically turn our primaries from *elections* into *selections*. This will mean that real conservatives will seldom get a chance to run in a general election, and the two parties will, over time, blend together. One reason I decided to stay in our Senate race was to resist this dangerous trend and, thus, protect the face-to-face appraisals that primaries offer.

For a candidate, each region of the state presents its own particular challenge. I got a much warmer reception in the Kansas City area than I expected since the city was a Democratic stronghold and most of the Republicans lived in the Kansas suburbs. My warm welcome was partly because of the fabulous work of our Kansas City coordinator, Heather Hall. She is sweeter than a rose and tougher than spring steel. These were swell people, and I made some lifetime friends.

The southwest part of Missouri is mostly conservative. One night, my coordinators, my wife, and I took a deer-dodging drive all the way across the state to a Lincoln Day event near Branson. When I got there, I learned that John Brunner had a plane to catch, so the organizers allowed him to speak first. From that point, the speakers proceeded according to the scope of the office they were running for, starting with the most local. Some twenty speakers later, I gave my talk to those stalwart enough to stay awake. Given the historical context of a Lincoln Day, I spoke about America's unique founding and our responsibility to our Creator to honor the Founders' commitment to life, liberty, and the pursuit of happiness. The speech went well. I then shook a lot of hands and headed out around 11 p.m. for the four-and-a-half-hour drive back to St. Louis County. Only later did I learn that the plane Brunner had to "catch" was his own private plane. I had a car to catch, our rental car. It was that kind of campaign.

As I traveled around to various county Lincoln Days and talked to a lot of good-hearted patriots, I found there were several points about the Republican Party that I believe it is critical to clarify. America has a two-party system, and this system works better than Europe's many fractured parties. Some conservatives through the years have advocated starting a third conservative party out of dissatisfaction with the Republicans. These people should take a lesson from, of all people, the communists.

In Minnesota, the communists tried to create a distinct communist political party. They put millions of Soviet dollars into the project, to no avail. Then they got smart. They figured it would be cheaper to take over the Democratic Party, which they more or less then did. On the national level, Sam Webb, the chairman of the Communist Party USA, was endorsing Obama's jobs plan and by 2012 was openly supporting his reelection bid. The moral for conservatives—if the Republican Party is too liberal for our tastes, we must change the party.

In my talks, I also emphasized that I believed it was destructive to criticize party leaders in the media. The liberal media welcome Republicans who will triangulate and tear down their own team. Senator McCain comes to mind for his repeated public attacks on his fellow Republicans, particularly. In contrast, as a congressman, I reserved my criticisms for Republican conferences, where I tried to be tactful, but direct and effective.

The southwest portion of Missouri presented a unique challenge for me. Romney got more than 60 percent of the vote in Greene County, where Springfield is located, and more than 70 percent in the surrounding counties. Southwest Missouri is the state's conservative stronghold. It is also the home base of Sen. Roy Blunt. Although Blunt and I always had a cordial enough relationship, he was cool to my candidacy from the beginning. This was surprising, because, unsolicited, I had endorsed his Senate race two years earlier.

During his race, Blunt frequently dropped my name to conservative groups around the state to garner support. Now when I was running, he was very reserved. I don't know why he was reserved, but it may have had something to do with the fact that we represent the two different strains of Republicans in Congress: those who put principles first and those who are pragmatic above all else. Blunt is good at politics, and his first obligation has always been to the party. In fact, he was appointed chief deputy whip after only one term in Congress and eventually became House majority whip.

In those positions, in spite of his claim to be a conservative, Blunt voted for bills like No Child Left Behind, Medicare Part D, the farm bills with all their social welfare, and TARP, the big bank bailout. He also was responsible for twisting arms to get other Republicans to vote the same way he did. My arm resisted his twisting.

Tea Party organizations were unmoved by Blunt's candidacy in 2010. After Blunt petitioned one group for its support, the group humorously headlined a poster, "Roy Blunt Pledges To Never Vote

Like Roy Blunt Again."[1] I will be the first to admit my own imperfections as a candidate, but I at least could promise that I *would be* able to vote the way I always had.

Politically minded and pragmatic as he was, Blunt and his people controlled the state Republican money and influence apparatus in 2012, especially in southwest Missouri. I had my work cut out for me to win that region on my own. Fortunately, we had the able assistance of Jonica and Michael Hope as regional leaders. Michael may have caught something, because he feels called to run for state representative.

Speaking of differences in the Republican Party brings up another common misconception. During the twelve years I worked with Republican members of Congress, I found most to be good-hearted people. We agreed on most issues about 85 percent of the time. I have frequently heard people say in disgust: "There is no difference between the parties." I understand their frustration, but there is, in fact, a chasm of difference between the parties:

| REPUBLICANS | DEMOCRATS |
| --- | --- |
| Believe in smaller and local government | Want ever-expanding federal government |
| Support 2nd Amendment | Want to confiscate guns |
| Mostly pro-life | Strongly pro-abortion |
| Believe in fiscal responsibility | Believe all problems solved by giving away more of other people's money |
| Start most meetings in prayer | Want to remove all public references to God; even voted whether to kick God out of the party platform! |
| Believe in free speech | Regulate speech by political correctness |
| Mostly pro-defense | Systematically dismantling and defunding past, present, and future military |

The Republican and Democratic platforms are vastly different. The point of disagreement within the Republican Party is largely tactical. The pragmatic politicians think politically and will not take a risk unless it benefits them or unless they can see a clear path to win. For them, winning is everything. Those motivated by principles place top priority on doing what is right, regardless of outcome. In our party, these are the serious conservatives. They will fight doggedly for the truth and for what is just. They tend to pull their motivation from their faith, believe they are called to do what is right, give their very best effort, and trust God for the results. Therefore, they are more willing to fight a battle that seems impossible to win, as many of us did with Obamacare.

In 1787, during the US Constitutional Convention, a delegate suggested that his colleagues cut some corners to make the new Constitution more politically palatable. George Washington, who as Speaker rarely took part in the debates, admonished, "Let us raise a standard to which the wise and honest can repair. The event is in the hand of God." This was a quote we printed on our campaign literature for more than twenty years. It pretty well summarizes a conservative view of tactics: do the right thing and trust the results to God Himself. Principle trumps politics.

If you remember, 2012 was the year the "Occupy" movement took center stage. We think of these people as "occupying Wall Street," where they at least got a little attention; but they were angry enough to even "occupy" places like St. Joseph and Springfield in Missouri. New Yorkers might take these people seriously. Missourians have much too much common sense to even fake an interest in the occupiers' pet peeves. I use the word "angry" for a reason. Often when these people confronted me, they did so aggressively and profanely. They seemed consumed with hatred and respected nothing. For the life of me I could not figure out what it was the occupiers hoped to accomplish. We had one thing in common: they didn't know either.

In Springfield, I ran into a cluster of more friendly "occupy"-

types who assumed the right to crash the privately sponsored meeting where I was asked to speak. They could do this because the talk was being held in the library, a public building. I had fun with the audience that day, just telling the great stories of America's founding. Every so often, I would give everyone in attendance a chance to vote. For example, I asked what the Pilgrims should have done in 1621 after almost half of them had died—go back to England on the *Mayflower* or stay?

Some of the occupiers said they liked what I had to say. It is likely that they had not before heard anything of the vision or principles of America's founding. Truth has a way of getting people's attention. The information that young people in particular receive is so tightly channeled that all they learn about conservatives is that they are supposed to hate them. As much as they denounce stereotypes, many liberals know nothing about conservatives other than the crude stereotypes they are fed on MSNBC or the pages of the *New Yorker*.

This ignorance has its comic underside. On one occasion, Brunner, Steelman, and I participated in a debate on the University of Missouri campus in Columbia. The front rows were crowded with enthusiastic supporters of mine. What the media did not know is that we had gotten the word to the Phi Gamma Delta boys that one of their fellow FIJIs was speaking, and they showed up in droves to cheer me on. I sure appreciated their warm support in an otherwise chilly, liberal city.

The debate moderator was a young grad student who was feeling a lot of pressure. He started by saying authoritatively, "We will proceed alphabetically." With almost a drum roll, he gave me the first shot at the question. "Congressman Akin," he said thoughtfully, "do you believe life begins at *contraception?*" Well, it's certainly not supposed to! This student was lucky he was not a Republican candidate. The media would have hung that paradoxical goof around his neck for the rest of his life.

As former senator George Allen will surely confirm, one thing that made the campaign trail more difficult and particularly more dangerous was the constant presence of Democrat "trackers." At almost every stop, there would be one and often two trackers. They would videotape everything. This meant that I had to be very careful because I tend to be a colorful speaker, and any single thing I said could be taken out of context and exploited. For this reason, the trackers guarantee cautious and boring presentations. The smarter local Republican leaders pick private meeting locations so the known trackers can be kept out. But in today's world of electronics, caution is the word.

Well into the summer, at a picnic in Sedalia, Missouri, one of our campaign staff talked to one of the top Democrat trackers, who volunteered, "You know that Akin is going to win, don't you?" My staffer responded, "Why do you think so?" The tracker said, "Akin will win because he is the candidate who knows what he believes." This may seem like a curious comment, but the tracker was talking about our message, our ability to connect the dots and to inspire people by explaining who we are as Americans.

Because I had more time to speak, my talk went something like this:

> In America, people are important because our Creator made each and every one of us. That's why people on September 11 gave their lives to rescue complete strangers; that's why our sons and daughters risk their lives for America. And not only did God make us very special, but He also prepared special work just for us. That is our destiny. Each day we must have the courage to live the dream God has put in our heart. The secret to America's greatness is that we acknowledged God as our Creator and Sustainer, as well as the Source of our liberties; America will only continue to be good by trusting Him with our hopes and dreams.
>
> Having hope centered in God helps us overcome the naysayers who have little faith or imagination: "It won't work." "You won't win." "Everyone will laugh at you." But it pays to recall that America was built by people others thought crazy, people crazy enough to cross an ocean to launch a civilization, crazy enough

to preserve that civilization even if it meant fighting the world's most powerful army, crazy enough to fight a civil war to perfect it. America was built one dream at a time by people of courage, allowed to have the freedom to make mistakes or to fail and pick back up to try again and again until succeeding—Thomas Edison, for instance, or Steve Jobs. And now more than ever, America needs each of us to have the courage to live our dreams, to bless our family and neighbors.

One place we can start is by stopping our federal government from stealing our freedom. Our freedom is stolen in taxes, in useless regulations, in laws that promote dependency, and in laws that allow outright killing. Without freedom, dreams remain dreams.

"Above all," I told the audience, "don't lose hope. As Patrick Henry observed, 'A just God presides over the destinies of nations.'"

My talks came from my heart because in running for the US Senate I was living what I was saying. On a number of stops, I felt that the dormant coals of patriotism and even revival were catching flame and that there was a strong, peaceful glow as our hearts were united as "one nation under God, indivisible, with liberty and justice for all"!

# 15

# REPUBLICAN PRIMARY HOME STRETCH: 2012

**B**y the time we got to June 2012, two months before the August primary, the polls had John Brunner in a slight lead, with Sarah Steelman and me hanging on not far behind. The fact that he had been on TV and radio for six months was paying dividends, but the battlefield was in flux. By July we could selectively run our own TV ads. Steelman had an ace up her sleeve and was about to play it, and to make matters interesting, Democratic senator McCaskill, flush with cash, decided to jump in as well.

Although all three candidates were running to the right, the difference between Brunner and me became clear in our final debate in July at Washington University in St. Louis. On the question of supporting a Romney administration, I said, "I'm going to wait and see what he does," and I then cited my opposition to George Bush initiatives, like No Child Left Behind and the bank bailout known as the TARP. I will support the Republicans but not when they abandon principle. Brunner, however, said he would follow Romney's lead.

In July, McCaskill started meddling in the Republican primary. Her people put together a series of ads with one seemingly directed against each of the three of us. The ad against Brunner, said *Politico* accurately, "undercut his conservative bona fides." The ad against Steelman chastised her for representing "more politics as usual."[1] The ad against me was the most nuanced. It seemed clear that McCaskill's people were building up my conservative credentials for the primary and exaggerating them in such a way as to scare Democrats and independents in the general election.

"Todd Akin, a crusader against bigger government," said the announcer. "Akin would completely eliminate the Departments of Education and Energy, and privatize Social Security."[2] The ad also quoted me describing President Obama as a "complete menace to our civilization."[3] That final quote has some truth to it, too, more now than ever.

The ad concluded, "Todd Akin—Missouri's true conservative is just too conservative."[4] Knowing that conservatives are more likely to vote in primaries, the McCaskill people were trying to throw the game my way. Some would debate this, but the give-away is that all the images they showed of me were friendly and positive. When trying to subvert a campaign, ad makers inevitably look for the harshest photos of the candidate they can find. McCaskill probably was afraid of Brunner's money and figured I'd be easier to demonize than Steelman.

The McCaskill camp would like to take credit for getting me elected, but when push came to shove, her ad did not put me over the top. After they ran I was still well behind Brunner, but there were still important tactical cards that had not been played.

One of those was that we finally had our own television ads running. Former Arkansas governor Mike Huckabee, who is very popular with Missouri Republicans, gave me a strong endorsement. He described me as "a Bible-based Christian," one who "supports traditional marriage, defends the unborn, and voted to defund Planned Parenthood."[5] He said, too, that my conservative credentials had been tested under fire in DC. This kind of talk made party leaders nervous, but it spoke to who I am and why I was running. There was nothing "stealth" about my campaign.

Like Britain in World War II, Steelman secured the most valuable of all allies. This was not one of Missouri's powerful Republicans but one of America's, Sarah Palin. In a TV commercial, Palin described Steelman as a "conservative maverick" who would fight for a constitutional amendment to force Congress to balance the budget. This was true enough on its own terms: Palin did not say, or imply, that Steelman was more conservative than her competitors. Her endorsement of Republicans in primaries in other states had been decisive and, therefore, attention getting.

ABC News reported on the Palin ad nine days before the August 7 primary. Reporter Chris Good acknowledged that John Brunner, who had spent nearly $7 million of his own money on the race and was backed by the US Chamber of Commerce, was still the favorite. Chris Good cited a recent Mason-Dixon poll conducted for the *St. Louis Post-Dispatch* that showed Brunner leading Steelman 33 percent to 27 percent. As far as the media knew, this was a two-person race, and I wasn't one of those persons. That same poll had me at 17 percent.[6]

If we lacked air power, our side did have something essential going for it—people who genuinely believed in what we were doing, Mike Huckabee among them. As the Sarah Palin ad made clear, Steelman, an economist by training, was positioning herself as an economic conservative, someone who would check excess spending and balance the budget. Brunner had staked out a very similar position. The two candidates only addressed social issues when they had to, and then cursorily. Economics was the national Republican message. It was important and easy to defend, with no messy social issues alienating the easily offended. I believed, however, that the Republicans' national message and Brunner's and Steelman's messages had a drawback—they were boring, and a boring message is a losing message. As I understood, and my core supporters did as well, our message evoked all that had been good, right, and true in America. It was an appeal for virtuous character, honesty, hard work, respect for others, and, of course, faith. It was an appeal for strong, happy families, and of course, it was an appeal for a limited government.

The questions I asked in 2012 are the questions we should be asking ourselves today, but with even more urgency. Do we treasure the gift our Creator bestowed on us of life, liberty, and the ability to pursue our own destinies? Or do we overlook the manifold failures of our current administration, their criminal activities, their reckless spending, and much more in order to secure whatever gifts the government can give us? In short, do we choose freedom or freebies? We can't have both.

Going into the final weekend of the race, we were still down in the polls, and few gave us a chance of coming in second, let alone winning. That Friday, Palin came to Missouri to stump for Steelman, and Brunner continued to bombard us both from the air. It was time to deploy a resource that both of the other candidates lacked—a grassroots army. Our people freely involved themselves in our "get-out-the-vote," or GOTV, campaign. In addition to many other activities, we had our supporters going to some church parking lots and leaving an attractive flyer on every windshield, stressing my support for life, for liberty, and for the traditional Christian values on which the nation was founded.

It should not have been necessary for us to remind church-goers of the election at hand and the issues involved. Their pastors should have been doing this all along. One reason that many do not, however, is the fear that preaching the practical applications of God's Word will somehow cost them their tax-exempt status. This fear is unfounded. In the sixty years the relevant tax code has been on the books, only one church has lost its tax-exempt status, that just for one day, and that for running a full-page ad paid for by the church, not for anything preached from the pulpit. This reason, in my experience, tends to be more of an excuse than a reason.

In any case, our leafleting turned out to be far more controversial than we had expected. Almost immediately, Perry was fielding two different kinds of calls. One kind came from pastors of certain churches who felt we were bringing politics to their church. The second type of call, and more numerous, came from citizens who were pleased to receive the information and who wanted to know how they could help. Perry politely apologized to the former and took the names and numbers of the latter. That flyer was a beautiful piece and had been written and typeset by my daughter Hannah, a senior art major at Hillsdale College. Later, when I got word of the hard feelings, I was saddened that many church leaders were afraid to stand up for the biblical principles that America so desperately needs to be taught.

Allow me to digress from our story briefly, because there is an issue here directly connected with America's survival. The reason most pastors don't deal with the great issues of our day is because people in churches can have strong opinions, and a pastor doesn't want to divide his or her church on some controversial question. These issues also require a lot of careful study, which takes time. It's much safer to give a dull sermon than a fiery one. Specifically, the problem comes in the definition of an "exegetical sermon." Today in most conservative churches, this means taking a biblical text and explaining what it says. Commonly, this results in making some theological point that is not wrong but also is not relevant.

Let me be totally clear, however—I believe God's Word is the only thing that belongs in the pulpit.

Here is the problem. In 2 Timothy 3:16–17 and in other places in the Bible, we see that the principles of scripture should guide people in how to live, how to raise families, and how to build a civilization. Almost every evangelical type of person would agree with this, but we don't do it.

If you attend a conservative church, do you see a number of children? Have you ever heard an exegetical sermon taken from the Bible explaining what the Bible says about education? Have you ever heard a sermon taken from Genesis comparing creation with evolution? In 1621, Governor Bradford spoke about the classical writers who advocated what we would call socialism "as if they were wiser than God." The Plymouth colonists thought it unbiblical and unworkable and rejected it before their first year was out.[7] Have you ever heard a sermon taken from biblical texts teaching how socialism is unbiblical and a form of theft?

We claim that the Bible gives us the principles to live by, but we refuse to study or teach them.

I bring this up here because millions of Americans are being savaged by bad ideas, and it is the duty of pulpits to protect them with truth. As it says in Hosea 4:6, "My people are destroyed for lack of knowledge."

Please review a few sermons from the late Rev. D. James Kennedy's website to get a good example of practical, passionate, and interesting preaching (particularly his sermon titled "The Bible and Economics").[8]

As we approached Election Day, my nineteen-year-old daughter, Abigail, had assumed the job of events coordinator during the campaign, and it was she who put together our election night party at the Columns conference center in St. Charles. We descended on the Columns that night not exactly confident, but hopeful. Primaries are always hard to call, and a tight three-way like this was even harder. Our campaign team tracked the results on a series of laptops down the hall while our anxious supporters gathered upstairs in the ballroom. As is often the case, the people in the "War Room" knew the outcome well before the media did.

Not long after the polls closed, Senator Blunt called my campaign strategist and said that based on the way key precincts were reporting, I was going to win. As they say, victory has a thousand fathers, and defeat is an orphan. Blunt had just adopted me. He would orphan me soon enough.

Like a brushfire, the buzz jumped around the room and then down the hall. Our supporters were hearing the rumor of victory in one room and the "too close to call" media chatter in the other. Preferring the rumor, they willed it to be true, and soon even the media caught on. When a local TV station announced that I had won, the room went crazy in a way that startled even the most cynical of campaign veterans. People I had barely even seen smile before were jumping up and down, yelling. Everyone told them we didn't have a chance, but somehow Team Akin had pulled it off.

Not only did we win, but we also beat our nearest opponent, John Brunner, by six percentage points, and he had outspent us four to one. Later polling showed that our multipronged GOTV, manned by local volunteers, had worked a miracle in the last days of the election. We had gained more than six points in just three days! Grass roots and message had beat money.

Lulli looked stunning that night, and I mostly just looked stunned. Our whole family joined us on the stage. When the moment came, it seemed natural for Lulli and me to raise joined hands in victory. Our supporters were as excited as we were. They knew what the pundits did not, that the best campaigns work from the ground up. They didn't vote for me because I was smart or handsome or charismatic. They voted for me because they had values in which they deeply believed and values they knew I shared.

There was a cyclone of energy in the room that night, a whirlwind of thankfulness, a collective answered prayer. In politics, I had never known a thrill quite like it. After a rousing, heartfelt ovation, I said to my supporters, "I would like to give thanks to God our Creator, who has blessed this campaign and heard your prayers and answered them with victory." Then I gave credit to those who took God's blessing and ran with it. "From the depths of my heart," I said, "I want to thank every single volunteer. Never in my life have I had such a fantastic team."[9]

I spoke for only another five minutes and laid out the respective philosophies of the two different camps. McCaskill believed in big government, big spending, and less liberty. I believed in less government, less spending, and more liberty. "The choice is clear," I said, and I meant it. This was more clarity, however, than the Democrats and their media allies could endure. We would hear from them soon enough, but for the moment, we enjoyed the wonderful gift we had just received from God. It felt good.

# 16

# DAMAGE CONTROL

The honeymoon was short lived, to say the least. What my family, staff, and I endured for the month after my Jaco interview was something very few people ever get a chance to experience. One moment you are a respected public servant with a scandal-free record dating back twenty-four years. The next moment, you are a national pariah and a pox on your own party—all just for saying a few misinterpreted words. How bizarre.

We certainly had no time to brood over the situation. Before dawn Monday morning, Perry and I caught a plane to Columbus, Ohio, the headquarters of "The Strategy Group Company." The organization is a full service political advertising shop started and run by Rex Elsass. Their mission is to get conservative candidates elected, and through the years, they have logged an incredible record of wins. For this, they are disliked and attacked by moderate Republican staffers and party bosses. The Strategy Group's specialty is television ads. I signed Rex onto our team in 2000, when I won Congress by fifty-six votes. Over the next twelve years, he did our campaign advertising for Congress, and he would stay with us all the way on our Senate run.

On arrival, Rex called his team together, and we all prayed. Rex is a good friend and fierce advocate. He stood shoulder to shoulder in our time of need, and in the days ahead he would stand up to the party bosses. Though they would threaten, he would never blink.

Several strategic decisions had to be made immediately. The first was whether we were going to apologize. Unlike some other candidates for political ridicule, I had done nothing for which I was ashamed. Yes, for sure, I could have phrased my answer better, but I had no apologies for the position I took on rape.

That much said, my key staff and virtually everyone I consulted wanted me to apologize publicly, so we cut a thirty-second TV spot to do just that. The spot began with a still image of Lulli and me and was followed by me speaking directly to the camera. Here is what I said:

> Rape is an evil act. I used the wrong words in the wrong way, and for that I apologize. As the father of two daughters, I want tough justice for predators. I have a compassionate heart for the victims of sexual assault. I pray for them. The fact is, rape can lead to pregnancy. The truth is, rape has many victims. The mistake I made was in the words I said, not in the heart I hold. I ask for your forgiveness.

Of all the people I consulted, only one told me I should not apologize. That one person was Lulli. In retrospect, I am inclined to agree with her. By asking the public at large for forgiveness, I was validating the willful misinterpretation of what I had said. I was also diverting a good chunk of our limited resources to advance a position—rape is evil—that no one disputed and that had almost nothing to do with the job of a US senator.

The second strategic decision focused on how to handle the national media, now in full feeding-frenzy mode. Because of our decision on the apology, we decided to answer any further questions on the subject by saying, "We have made our apology, and we are not going back over old ground." This we believed would, over time, allow us to go on to more favorable subjects. I stuck to this media discipline closely, and it helped some, but there was blood in the water, and I was the bait.

We scheduled two interviews we hoped would be friendly. Hannity savaged us right off the bat by harping on the view that we could never win. I explained that I had heard that many times before some of my elections, and we were only two weeks past a primary we were also not supposed to win.[1]

Mike Huckabee was a real gentleman and allowed me to explain our position. He asked tough but reasonable questions. I got the sense that he had had liberals gang up against him, and he understood how it felt. "I'm not a quitter," I told Huckabee. "By the grace of God, we're going to win this race."[2] God may have had other plans about the outcome, but for the moment, I felt confident He wanted me to stay in the race.

During this time Lulli was at home alone with all kinds of media people coming to our front door and roaming our front yard. This was a concern because of the threats we'd received that were being investigated by the FBI. The generally liberal *New York* magazine reported accurately, "The Office of Congressman Akin has received threats of rape of his official staff, family, and the congressman himself along with suggestions that individuals should die."[3] Though the liberal media would mock this, the police thought the threats serious enough to provide round-the-clock surveillance of our house for more than a week. Lulli slipped out with great staffer Jonathan Carman to an undisclosed location.

The media provided the surveillance for our campaign office. By Monday of that week, every major station in the St. Louis area had a truck parked outside the office, as did stations from Kansas City and Springfield. The phones of all our key staff started ringing Sunday and never stopped. The pressure was unrelenting.

With Perry and me gone, Ryan Hite, only twenty-three years old, had to take the lead on media communications. For a week of sixteen-plus-hour days, he had to field demands and questions for which he literally had no answers. Ryan is young, smart, and tough, but playing javelin catcher for a US Senate campaign under siege was above and beyond the call of duty. At particularly difficult moments, a wonderful young lady, Alaina Carman, offered a calm, orderliness to the HQ chaos, and encouragement. It was the start of something special. She and Ryan married in the spring of 2014. God uses all kinds of situations to get people's attention.

After cutting the apology ad, we took time to prepare for facing the major media. On Wednesday morning of my first week as a household name, I did a live remote with George Stephanopoulos on ABC's *Good Morning America*. Those who coach media will tell you that there is nothing harder to do than stare at a camera and pretend that you are having a real conversation. Our rehearsals worked well enough. I appeared calm, looked sane, and kept relentlessly on message.[4]

When Stephanopoulos asked whether I was staying in the race despite the opposition from my own party, I said, "I have made the decision to stay in because we can win." I meant what I said. I rejected his suggestion that the race was lost and explained that the clear difference in positions between me and McCaskill made it winnable. I also made the point that party voters had made a decision, and that it was not right for party bosses to overturn it.

Sticking to the talking points, with regards to the *Jaco Report* remarks, I would apologize for the coupling of the words "legitimate" and "rape" and admit to being "medically wrong" on the subject of pregnancy. I gave too much away, but I didn't want our whole campaign to be about abortions for raped women, so I didn't argue the several points. In retrospect, I would like to have explored the effect of stress on pregnancy, but a five-minute segment on *Good Morning America* was not the place. In a similar vein, I chose not to question whether all rape accusations were "legitimate," although Stephanopoulos opened the door by talking about Norma McCorvey. I may have been a little too much on message to take that opening.

One point I was able to reaffirm was that I was not apologetic at all about being pro-life. For his part, Stephanopoulos, like almost everyone else in the media, avoided the issue at the heart of the controversy, namely, whether a baby conceived in rape deserved the same chance at life as any other baby. This was an argument that, if pressed, I would have won. Stephanopoulos, a former Clinton operative, preferred to talk about self-destructive Republican politics rather than anything of substance. For a Democrat, this was a much more fruitful discussion thread.

I cannot imagine that my appearance on *Good Morning America* or, later that morning, on the *Today* show had much effect on the outcome of the race. It did, however, put party bosses on notice that I was still planning on staying in the race. They had already informed me that I would be as welcome at the upcoming Republican Convention in Tampa as Hurricane Isaac. Stephanopoulos gleefully alerted his audience to that unhappy fact.

Missouri Republicans are not nearly as pliable as Missouri Democrats. They are only half as likely to vote straight ticket, and they never would have voted, as Democrats did in 2000, for a candidate who had died with the understanding that his wife would fill the position.

No, the reality was that I stood a better chance of winning at this stage than any other Republican. If I withdrew, whichever candidate the party picked would have earned the resentment of scores of thousands of Missouri Republicans. The compensatory honeymoon that this candidate would have enjoyed from the media would not have lasted a full news cycle. Ask veteran Democrats how well they fared when their party unceremoniously dumped Missourian Tom Eagleton from the national ticket in 1972 for a party insider and Kennedy crony. If my memory serves me, the McGovern–Shriver ticket carried one state. Also, in Missouri, the general election is only three months after the primary! Although not as tight as Massachusetts with only two months, it makes it very hard to remove an incumbent if there is a long, hard-fought primary battle.

Following my Wednesday morning TV appearances, I stayed away from the media until a press conference late that Friday afternoon in suburban St. Louis. It was held in a meeting hall for home educators near our campaign headquarters. After the press had gathered, I entered directly from the parking lot through a back door. I felt as relaxed and as at ease as I had any time during the campaign. I think that my demeanor disappointed the many reporters present. They were hoping, I suspect, for more drama, more anger, even. The speech I gave lasted only about a minute. As temperate as it was, it still must have unnerved the Beltway bosses.

"Good afternoon and thank you all for coming out," I began. "Apparently, there are some people who are having trouble understanding our message. We are going to be here through the November election, and we are here to win." I then laid out the difference in vision between our campaign and McCaskill's. The America I represented promised more freedom, more jobs, less bureaucracy, less big government, less taxes, and a bright hope for the future. McCaskill's America promised just the opposite on every point, as well as "the same stalled economy" we had been enduring since Obama took office. That was pretty much the whole speech. As stark as the differences may have seemed, I was not exaggerating.

Perry limited the follow-up to five questions. As I sensed then, and can see even more clearly now in watching the video, the reporters provided all the tension in the room. Neither they nor I expected to find ourselves center stage in a high-profile political melodrama, but I had already been getting used to it for a week. They had not. The first reporter asked me about the anguish I must have felt this past week and the sleepless nights I must have experienced. A second asked about the threats made against my family, especially my wife and daughters. A third asked about the pressure I was getting from Republicans to drop out. A fourth asked me about whether we could hope to run a normal campaign.

As I calmly explained, we had been working for the last fifteen months without the support of the party. I had never been its favorite candidate. That was not about to change, certainly not for the better. No one gave us much hope of winning the primary, but we won by six points by taking the campaign to the people, which I promised to continue to do. "This is an *election*," I reminded the reporters in the room and the Republican bigwigs back in Washington, "not a *selection*." As to the threats, they were real enough to engage the FBI, and as to the pressure, that, too, was real, but sticking to principle eased it considerably. Besides, Perry had been doing his best to screen me from the torrent of abusive communications. I did, however, concede with a smile, "We have been busy."

Although this remark drew the day's only laughter, there was some amusing comedy afoot. Given the threats in the air, we had a police presence at the press conference. In addition, several of our staffers with concealed carry permits were carrying. To distinguish those individuals, we put green dots on their name tags and alerted the police to the same. On seeing the green dots, however, one of our junior staffers assumed that all of the staff, male and female, were supposed to have green dots and made sure that everyone got one. The police must have thought we were about to defend the Alamo. As far as I know, no one clued them in on all the extra green dots.

# 17

# PLAYING HARDBALL

Looking back at that first week, we saw the number of online hits for "Todd Akin" go from two thousand Sunday night to more than two billion by the following Tuesday. Like "climate change," this was an artificial maelstrom created and sustained to promote a socialist agenda.

It is important for all conservatives and patriots to understand the formidable strategy that liberals have adapted from Saul Alinsky's playbook, *Rules for Radicals*. It works like this: Democrats and their allies have trackers stalk the campaign of every significant Republican. They record everything said in public and/or sometimes even in private, as was the case in Mitt Romney's "47 percent" remark. If a Republican says anything that can possibly be interpreted as inappropriate, the trackers feed the remark to the left-leaning Beltway blogs, which in turn feed it to the major media.

At an August 2006 campaign stop, Virginia Republican senator George Allen called out one of the trackers. "This fellow here, over here with the yellow shirt, Macaca, or whatever his name is. He's with my opponent," said Allen. "Let's give a welcome to Macaca, here. Welcome to America and the real world of Virginia." The tracker was of Indian descent. He and his allies in the media pounced on Allen's remark and denounced him to the world as a racist, even though Allen *thought* he was using a made-up word when he called the man Macaca. He could not possibly have known that, in the Portuguese language at least, the word means "monkey." Allen is not Portuguese . . . and neither was his opponent. Although Allen's remark was not nearly the gaffe Biden's was on the subject of Indians, Allen never recovered and lost his reelection bid.[1]

This strategy, I repeat, is designed to punish Republicans. In its particulars, it goes something like this:

(1) Liberal groups select something that has been done or said that can be misunderstood or misquoted so as to create resentment and controversy.

(2) They intentionally misrepresent the meaning of what was said or meant.

(3) They act outraged and deeply offended.

(4) They urge all in their group to actively participate in their verbal stoning party.

(5) They corner public figures and ask them if they are as outraged as everyone else.

(6) They get the target to apologize, then reject the apology as not sincere enough.

(7) The chattering class in the media blindly throws verbal stones without asking why.

(8) The instigators add additional lies upon the target's original statement to further isolate and demonize him.

(9) They keep the whole process going in the media as long as possible.

(10) When such a verbal stone-throwing is successful, the instigators have: eliminated an opponent, taught followers to obey, and coined a poison label to stick on future opponents.

This process requires lying, bearing false witness, and intentionally destroying the reputation of an innocent person and possibly his or her family, but for those who support the willful killing of innocents in the womb, libel and slander are a piece of cake.

To work well, this kind of character assassination must satisfy four criteria. The perpetrators need the seed of some comment or action that can be possibly misunderstood. They need a media that will reliably stoke the furor. They need gullible voters as well as media people not savvy enough to ask, "What did the victim actually say?" Lastly, it is also helpful if a willing Republican leadership is anxious to get rid of a candidate who is not an obedient team player.

This backdrop suggests some steps that could have been taken to lessen the impact of their hit job on our campaign. For one, I could have given them a smaller target. I might have said, for instance, "No, Charles, abortion should not be legal in the case of rape. I know how traumatic rape must be for the victim, but if we were to punish someone for this crime, it should be the rapist, not the baby, who is as deserving of life as any one of us."

This answer would still have created a firestorm, but it would have been much less of one if we as a party had a consistent position on abortion. Unfortunately, many of my fellow pro-life Republicans, including Mitt Romney, have argued for a "rape and incest" exception to an abortion ban. They may say that all life is precious, that life begins at conception, that abortion is murder, but if a baby comes into this world through rape or incest, they argue, then it is okay to take the life of that entirely innocent unborn child. These "exceptions" makes no sense morally or logically, no sense at all.

Yes, politically, opposing abortion in all circumstances remains a losing stance. But this is true because pro-life politicians and editorialists consistently fail to make the case for a coherent ban on abortion with an exception only for the life of the mother. By staying mum on the issue, or by arguing for other exceptions, fair-weather pro-lifers have left consistent pro-life candidates like Sharron Angle, Richard Mourdock, and me exposed to ridicule as extremists.

In addition to Republicans holding their ground on a principle, the Democrats need to be called to account for their hypocrisy. For example, Barack Obama wasted no time attacking me as well. But in his attack he ignored the abortion issue and focused exclusively on my "legitimate rape" comment. From a political perspective, I hardly blame him for evading the issue of abortion. His record on the same is uniquely appalling. In 2002, Illinois state senator Obama voted against the Induced Birth Infant Liability Act, a bill that would have protected the life of any baby that survived a late-term abortion. When it was brought to his attention that certain abortion doctors might let babies die for ideological reasons, Obama answered, "What we are doing here is to create one more burden on a woman, and I can't support that."[2] That "burden" of which he spoke was a baby already alive outside the womb. And I'm the extremist?

With a more open discussion of abortion, my use of the word *legitimate* wouldn't have seemed unusual, let alone hurtful. Americans would have understood that some claims of rape are not legitimate, including the most consequential "rape" case in American history—*Roe v. Wade.* For those not familiar with the background to this case, the state of Texas in 1969 allowed abortion in the case of rape, but to be eligible for an abortion then, the victim had to produce the necessary police or medical validation. Given that abortion meant the taking of a human life, Texas took that validation seriously. Hoping to qualify for an abortion, Norma McCorvey told authorities that she had been raped, but she lacked any proof. Her request was denied.

Attorneys Linda Coffee and Sarah Weddington proved less scrupulous than the Texas authorities. They needed someone to play the role of "Jane Roe" in the case they were bringing against all abortion law. As McCorvey, now an ardent pro-lifer, would later admit, she was lying, but the attorneys had no great interest in the truth. That one lie wrought the infamous *Roe v. Wade* decision, the Supreme Court's greatest assault on civil rights since Dred Scott, and a death sentence for some fifty-six million unborn babies.

Overall, the *Roe v. Wade* decision rested on three tortured premises. First, as with Dred Scott, the justices denied personhood to a whole class of humanity. Second, they made a legislative decision that, as justices, they were constitutionally not authorized to make. And third, they left unchallenged McCorvey's lies about having been raped.[3]

In recent years, another notorious rape case proved to be illegitimate as well. In March 2006, in Durham County, North Carolina, District Attorney Michael Nifong was in a desperate race to retain his job. To strengthen his hold on the black vote, he allowed a rape accusation by a black female against three Duke University lacrosse players to move forward despite the fact that all the evidence he had gathered pointed to the players' innocence. After a great deal of private grief and public humiliation, the players were exonerated. As to Nifong, his reckless ambition cost him his job, his law license, and his reputation.

Rape is a horrible crime. I have zero sympathy for those who commit it. For this reason, if I had been in Congress in 1998, I would have voted with my colleagues to impeach President Bill Clinton. I am sure there are people reading this right now wondering what kind of connection I am going to make, but please bear with me. I take no joy in telling this story, but it is essential if we are to understand how Democrats and the media exploit the good manners and courtesy of Republicans.

Known in government documents as "Jane Doe No. 5," Juanita Broaddrick made a highly credible claim that Bill Clinton had raped her when he was attorney general of the state of Arkansas. "It was a real panicky, panicky situation," Broaddrick would tell Lisa Myers on NBC's *Dateline* in February 1999. "I was even to the point where I was getting very noisy, you know, yelling to 'Please stop.' And that's when he pressed down on my right shoulder and he would bite my lip." On the way out of the room, when Clinton saw her swollen lip, he famously said, "You better get some ice on that."[4] It was Broaddrick's testimony under oath in the Paula Jones investigation that persuaded a few key congressmen to proceed with impeachment proceedings against Clinton.

Nor was Broaddrick the only woman to accuse Clinton of sexual assault, sexual indecency, or even of biting her lip to coerce sex. His gross misbehavior with Paula Jones led to the lawsuit that exposed his indecent White House carousing with intern Monica Lewinsky. Hillary Clinton's role in all of this was to manage what the Clinton camp called "bimbo eruptions"[5] and denounce women like Lewinsky and former Clinton girlfriend Gennifer Flowers as liars. I raise the issue of the Clintons' history because, as I mentioned in the first chapter, two weeks after the Jaco show, Bill Clinton would be taking center stage as keynote speaker at a Democratic National Convention whose subtext was to be the "Republican War on Women."

In August 2012, this was all common knowledge. So when the media came to Romney for a response to my comments on the Jaco show, he might have said the following: "A credibly accused rapist is giving the keynote speech at the Democratic convention in two weeks, and you want me to denounce a decent, God-fearing man for his inelegant comments about rape? No, not happening, and if the truth hurts, put some ice on it."

Mitt Romney is a gentleman. I understand that and respect it. But when the future of the nation is at stake and you're the heavyweight in the room, you sometimes have to take the gloves off and hit back with facts. He or his proxies might also have spoken to the Left's easy acceptance of director Roman Polanski's drugging and rape of a thirteen-year-old, after which he fled the country. This did not stop the liberal worthies of Hollywood from giving the fugitive rapist a standing ovation in 2003 when Polanski received a best-director Oscar Award in absentia. Days before the Oscars, Patrick Goldstein of the *Los Angeles Times* questioned whether "an artist's accomplishments should be judged against his misdeeds."[6] Misdeeds? In the same article actor and Democratic activist Warren Beatty called the rape a "personal mistake." Mistake? No. Putting dark clothes in the laundry with whites is a mistake. Putting regular fuel in a diesel tank is a mistake. Raping a drugged thirteen-year-old is a crime that cannot be justified or excused.

Actress and Democratic activist Whoopi Goldberg apparently thought otherwise. In 2009, she clarified Polanski's crime on *The View*. "I know it wasn't rape-rape. It was something else but I don't believe it was rape-rape," said Goldberg. "He went to jail and when they let him out he was like, 'You know what, this guy's going to give me a hundred years in jail. I'm not staying.' So that's why he left."[7] Whoopi's career suffered not a bit.

Going forward, Republicans must come to grips with the fact that the political left and their media allies use sex as a weapon against the political right. There are no objective standards, no rules, no courts of appeal. The same people who expressed horror at the unfounded accusation that Supreme Court nominee Clarence Thomas told dirty jokes cheered wildly as a serial sexual predator keynoted their convention. The same people who denounced Rush Limbaugh for calling Sandra Fluke a slut turned a blind eye to their own Bill Maher when he called Sarah Palin a word we can't even print. Space permitting, I could cite a score more prominent examples of this preposterous double standard.

If Romney or his people had pointed out the hypocrisy of the Democrats' fake outrage over my remarks, as several bloggers did, he could have put the brakes on the "war on women" nonsense, thrown the Democrats on the defensive, and possibly captured the presidency. Unfortunately, Romney did the opposite. Within twenty-four hours of the airing of the Jaco show, he told the media: "Congressman Akin's comments on rape are insulting, inexcusable and, frankly, wrong. Like millions of other Americans, we found them to be offensive."[8] Thanks, Mitt.

With Republican leadership condemning me, the Democrats

felt free to lie about what I said. Soon after Romney's comments, the Obama campaign, in the person of the suddenly famous contraceptive champion Sandra Fluke, sent an e-mail to millions of Americans under the heading, "Legitimate Rape." "Akin," she said, "thinks that victims of 'legitimate rape' don't get pregnant because 'the female body has ways to try to shut that whole thing down'?"[9] I actually said that the body *tries* to reject impregnation but that it doesn't always succeed. The Obama people changed my "rarely" to "never."[10] With the Republicans cowering, they had no fear of lying about "misdeeds" like "rape-rape."

During this first week, while I was being pilloried by friend and foe alike, it was becoming increasingly apparent that still another strategic decision was pending. By the time I talked to former Arkansas governor Mike Huckabee live on his radio show on Monday, the state and national parties were quietly letting it be known that they wanted me out of the race. As the law was interpreted, if I withdrew within two weeks of the primary date—that is the Tuesday after the Jaco show—the Republican Party could replace me without needing judicial approval.

John Cornyn, the head of the National Republican Senatorial Committee, was quick to go on record with a not-too-subtle suggestion that I withdraw. "I recognize this is a difficult time for him," Cornyn said in a statement on that Monday, "but over the next twenty-four hours, Congressman Akin should carefully consider what is best for him, his family, the Republican Party, and the values that he cares about and has fought for throughout his career in public service."[11]

If nothing else, the plot to vilify me had raised my national profile overnight in ways that no positive accomplishment ever could have. On the plus side, many pro-lifers from across the country saw through my semantic tics to the substance of what I had to say and agreed with me. Contributions, mostly small, began to pour in to our website. There was no way I could match the $20 million that Claire McCaskill eventually raised, but we would raise just enough to get our message out. Unlike many of McCaskill's major donors, these contributors wanted no more from me than that I stick to my principles and the godly principles of our nation's founding, to life, liberty, and the pursuit of happiness. That I was prepared to do.

I don't pretend to be any more stalwart than the average person. I know that whatever courage I do have comes from my faith. The God whom I serve is much bigger than all the party bosses, media bullies, and Democratic operatives combined. That is why I was less anxious than I might have otherwise been. When I woke in a sweat in the middle of the night, I was never alone, not even on the road. In the most humble motel, in the most obscure town in Missouri, God was always there with me. Many a restless night I prayed, "Lord, I am carrying too much weight. Help me bear it." He never disappointed. He never does.

# 18

# PILING ON

The Republican leadership has ways to help people "understand" what the right decision is. Early in the week following the Jaco interview, I called Sen. Roy Blunt. I suggested to him that I knew that some people would be calling for me to step down. However, for the sake of party unity, as well as relations between the two of us, I suggested that it would be better if he stayed uninvolved. From his own perspective, it would be a lousy strategy for Blunt to place himself between the moderates and conservatives of Missouri's Republican Party.

That evening, we received his reply—a letter that was to be soon released if I did not step down. It called for my withdrawal and was signed by every current and past Republican US senator from Missouri. Some signatures hurt. This was the opening salvo of a well-organized, full-scale Republican attack, led in most cases by the state party that worked under Roy Blunt's direction.

As I mentioned previously, Roy Blunt is good at politics and usually tries not to leave fingerprints on his handiwork. This time he would leave a bloody war club with his fingerprints all over it. Thus began what would turn out to be a unique aspect of our race.

We were fighting both parties, a war on two fronts.

For a variety of bad reasons, the National Republican Party lined up with Barack Obama criticizing me. In fact, just about every Republican with access to a microphone made a beeline to it. Sen. John McCain called my remarks "idiotic." Sen. Mitch McConnell called them "inexcusable." To Sen. Susan Collins, they were merely "bizarre." Hawaii governor Linda Lingle denounced them as "reprehensible." The normally prudent Charles Krauthammer called them "toxic." Michelle Malkin dismissed them as "ignorant," and young female commentator S. E. Cupp ridiculed them as "utter nonsense." In an age when everything gets recorded, I knew these anxious denunciations would come back to haunt me, and I was right.

You will start to see a pattern here. My critics called my comments "outrageous," but they would not say what it was about my comments that outraged them. As Republicans, we do not advance our cause by shooting our wounded. In this situation, a prudent answer to a question about my comments might have been: "I didn't hear Akin's words. What exactly did he say that some think offensive?" This kind of query would have blown the cover on intentional misrepresentation.

Unfortunately, that is not how Republicans responded. I guess they thought that if you can't beat the media, why bother to try? This is classic moderate thinking. The National Republican Senatorial Committee (NRSC) staff put this self-defeating strategy into action. Each day, its staffers clipped all the negative articles about me in the media and sent them to our office. Their message, of course, was, *you can't win*. Useful as it was as a clipping service, in every other way the NRSC undermined our efforts.

One particular trick that some wily Republican operative played on us was to share my personal cell phone number nationally. From then on, the phone was about as helpful to me as it was on September 11. Other party-inspired mischief was even less helpful. One of the biggest jobs of a candidate is to raise money. This requires making endless calls to possible donors. Once the smoke had cleared a little, I started to call some of the St. Louis donors who had stood by me in the past, some for more than twenty years. Boy, did I get an earful. As I learned, the party had contacted most of these people and turned them against us. The strategy was obvious: starve a campaign of money and it will collapse like one of the twin towers.

It was about this time that I received the bad news of another Republican kick in the shins. The president of a small coal company was a great patriot and had done a fantastic fund-raising event for me in the primary. (As an aside, this executive really fought for clean coal and put the executives of big coal companies to shame by his zeal.) He had agreed to do an even bigger event for me in the general election. We had agreed to a date, and I had every reason to believe we could raise between $350,000 and $400,000. This was a very big deal for us. Unfortunately, I had mentioned this event to Sen. Roy Blunt previously. You guessed it, the event was cancelled. When I called the president of the coal company, he confirmed my suspicions. He had been contacted by the party.

Had it not been for the numerous small contributions from patriots across America, the campaign would have collapsed at the starting gate.

In addition to going after our dollar base, the Roy Blunt machine went after our employees. It was reported to me that many of our official congressional staff as well as our campaign staff had been getting phone calls. One of our employees received a threat from a ranking state party official reckless enough to put it into writing. It reads as follows:

Dear XXXXX,

There is no way Mr. Akin can win this election, and his selfish and stubborn resistance to the will of the Republican Party, both in Missouri and nationally, will come at a high price. If he does not withdraw from this race we are conceding victory to Claire McCaskill. I do not want to see your future in Missouri politics tarnished, and if you continue to support Mr. Akin's bid for senate by working on his campaign, the MRP will have no choice but to refuse support for any future political endeavors you may have. I hope you consider the gravity of the situation and choose your path accordingly.

For young professional people working to get a foothold in the political world, these threats were very sobering. A combination of long hours, media attacks, threats of being killed or raped, and now promises to ruin careers began to take their toll. Perry had to counsel our staff who were hurting, even as he and his family had to deal with their own concerns. Despite the efforts of our foes—and our *friends*—all but one DC staffer opted to stay true to the end. Perhaps you can see why, when it was all over, I made the statement that this was the finest team I have ever been fortunate enough to work with.

The intensity of the attacks pushed our outstanding and loyal field director, Peter Williams, to the edge. He recalls attending a meeting of skeptical North St. Louis County Republicans that first week as a proxy for me. Initially, the group, like many he spoke to, was resistant. But as he recounted the horrors of the last few days, his emotionally wrought testimony changed the mood of the whole room. These people could see for themselves how unmerciful and unfair the assault on our campaign had been, and they started writing checks for Todd Akin for Senate.

Our vendors also reported calls from the party, but to their credit all of them except one stuck with us. In addition, some of our more nationally prominent conservative supporters were also receiving calls from the NRSC and sitting senators, asking them to drop their support of our campaign.

If nothing else, the party is thorough. David Lane got a sense of this up close. David Lane is the enthusiastic organizer of major events all over America called "Pastors and Pews." Dave received a call from Rob Jesmer, NRSC's executive director. Rob wanted Dave to persuade as many pastors as possible to sign a letter asking me to step down. Rob offered to reimburse Dave for his efforts. David Lane told Jesmer no in forceful but Christian terms.

I did not speak of these efforts to sabotage our team during the campaign, because I feared the party in Missouri would be further divided going into an important election. Unfortunately, Karl Rove, American Crossroads, and other moderates have openly stated that they will work for their preferred candidates and take down the principled conservative in primaries. I fear what happened to me will happen to many others.

As I mentioned before, we were a campaign fighting on two fronts. The Democrats we understand. For years, they and their media have tended to divide all Republicans into two categories, the most dominant category being "idiot." In their book, the Democrats characterize Dwight Eisenhower as intellectually incurious, even simple-mined, even though he orchestrated Operation Overlord, the World War II Battle for Normandy. Gerald Ford, the White House's best athlete ever, couldn't walk across the room without tripping. Ronald Reagan, the man who took down the Soviet empire, was an "amiable dunce." A grocery scanner was smarter than the senior George Bush. Dan Quayle couldn't spell "potato." George W. Bush came from the village in Texas that was "missing its idiot." So, at least, said the bumper stickers. And Sarah Palin could allegedly "see Russia from my house," even though she never said any such thing.

The media had just ushered me into the "stumbling idiot" hall of fame. Given the presence there already of an "amiable dunce" like Ronald Reagan, I did not bother to take much offense.

The second allowable Republican category was that of "evil genius," the reigning king of which was strategist Karl Rove, and his heir apparent seemed to be RNC chairman and boy genius Reince Priebus. I will leave the "evil" discussion to others. What I want to challenge is the "genius" part of the equation.

On the first morning of the Republican Convention in Tampa, just two days after my St. Louis press conference, Priebus spoke on camera to bloggers Ben Howe and Chris Loesch. A forty-year-old Wisconsin attorney with ties to Gov. Scott Walker, Priebus had run for elected office on his own only once and lost. That was for a state senate seat in Wisconsin. Priebus worked his way up through Wisconsin's Republican ranks before taking over as RNC's general counsel in 2009. In 2011, the party elected him chairman. In his scramble for the chair, Priebus seemed to have learned little about the art of discretion.

When the bloggers asked him about Missouri, Priebus went into this elaborate song and dance about how he took the job as chair because he was "worried about the future of the country." As he saw it, I was apparently not "in it for the cause."[1] I cared more about my own prospects than I did the good of the country, proof of which was that I had not dropped out and let that mythical person with a better chance of winning carry the Republican banner forward.

After urging me "to step aside," a preposterous request two days after my rather definitive press conference, Priebus showed his incredible inconsistency with his final comment. In response to a question as to whether the RNC position on me would change if I stayed in the race, he said for the ages, "No, no, no. He can be tied. We're not going to send him a penny."[2] Was he not aware how contradictory his comments were? A second ago, he was saying, "That is all this is about, putting your country first." His whole argument was that I should drop out because I could not win. Now he was saying, even if I could win, the RNC still would do nothing to help me. This was "putting your country first"?

Not only would the RNC not help me, but they would also do what they could to hurt me. This Karl Rove made clear on the final morning of the Republican Convention when he addressed a group of about seventy of the party's wealthiest and most powerful donors.

Unlike Romney, who made his impolitic remarks about the unswerving 47 percent in a closed setting, Rove knew there was at least one reporter present at the exclusive Tampa Club. That was Sheelah Kolhatkar of *Bloomberg Business Week*.

After some preliminary remarks by others, including Florida senator Marco Rubio, Rove and former Mississippi governor Haley Barbour talked inside baseball about the Republican strategy for winning back the White House.

Most of what Rove said was unremarkable. To Kolhatkar, he seemed more interested in strategy for its own sake than in the virtues of Mitt Romney. When it came to the Senate races, however, she described his analysis as "technical and masterly." According to Rove, I represented the greatest liability the Republicans faced in retaking the Senate. Wrote Kolhatkar, "Rove urged every attendee to apply pressure on Akin to convince him to leave the race." She then quoted Rove directly as saying, "We have five people who are interested" in replacing Akin. "We don't care who the nominee is, other than get Akin out."[3]

This, of course, was provocative enough, but Rove, never much of a comedian, saw fit to joke, "We should sink Todd Akin. If he's found mysteriously murdered, don't look for my whereabouts!"[4] Kolhatkar, understandably, put the joke in her opening paragraph. The influential Beltway publication, *Politico,* headlined its account of the fund-raiser, "Report: Karl Rove make [*sic*] Todd Akin murder joke."[5] From there, the news spread like head lice in a crowded country school.

Now, I never pretended to be a political genius. I never presumed that I was above making a gaffe. But you would think that the party's reigning big brains would have known better than to say something so boneheaded, especially when denouncing me for being boneheaded. Did they not stop to think how insulting these remarks would sound to the millions of social conservatives who distrust the Republican establishment to begin with and who actively dislike Rove himself? I have heard from literally hundreds of Republican voters who have told me that they would continue to donate to individual candidates but that they would never give to the party again. "Masterly"?

The irony, of course, is that I rarely deviated from the path chosen by the Republican leadership in Congress. I was not a maverick. I was not considered high maintenance. I raised considerable money for the campaigns of other Republicans. When I did resist the leadership it was because the leadership was straying from conservative principles hammered out time after time in party platforms.

Those Republicans who deviated to the left suffered no such criticism. Take my former colleague Mike Castle from Delaware. While serving in the House, he routinely scored the lowest of all members of the Republican caucus not only on social issues but also on economic ones. In 2008, for instance, he received a 26 percent rating from the Club for Growth. He received many an F from the NRA and a 0 percent from the National Right to Life.

Yet in 2010, when Castle ran for an open Senate seat in Delaware against conservative Christine O'Donnell, Rove and the Republican establishment supported Castle. They thought him more "electable." But if Castle were going to vote like a Democrat, what was the point of electing him at all? The Republican base understood this and chose O'Donnell. Rove was not a happy camper. On the night of O'Donnell's primary victory, he proceeded to sabotage her general election campaign. "There were a lot of nutty things she has been saying that don't add up," Rove told Sean Hannity and then proceeded to spell some of them out. Hannity described the allegation against O'Donnell as "trumped up" and summarized Rove's take on the nominee: "Sounds like you don't support her." Said Rove, "I'm for the Republican," but after he trashed O'Donnell on national TV, no one much believed him.[6]

Speaking of saying nutty things, Rove did contact me to apologize, at least after a fashion. At the time, I was at dinner in a small Kansas City restaurant with about a dozen staff and supporters. I took the call. From what I sensed, Rove was apologizing less for saying what he'd said than for getting caught saying it. I gave him my word that I would not cause any trouble in the ranks and then reassured him, "All of us say things that we wish we had not said." I enjoyed the irony of it all too much to get mad.

# 19

# FIRING BACK

Never will I leave you; never will I forsake you.
—Hebrews 13:5 NIV

Although many national and local Republicans treated our campaign like a mobile leper colony, there were some courageous enough to stand up. One was Newt Gingrich, the former Speaker of the House and very recently a serious presidential candidate. Right after the primary, he lent our campaign his media guy, the highly competent Rick Tyler. Also on *Meet the Press*, immediately after the Convention, Newt did not hesitate to call out Karl Rove. "In the age of Gabby Giffords, it is not a joke to say a member of Congress ought to get murdered," said Gingrich pointedly. On that same show, Gingrich defended my decision to stay in the race. "I think Todd Akin was the choice of the people in Missouri, and Todd Akin has publicly apologized," he said. "I just think people ought to be a little cautious about saying the voters of Missouri don't count."[1]

Gingrich made several trips to Missouri to support our campaign. On one occasion in late September, as we approached the drop-dead deadline for me to withdraw from the race, Gingrich joined me at a rally at the Kirkwood train station near St. Louis and for a fund-raiser shortly thereafter. Newt backed me up. "Todd Akin is a key to our winning control of the Senate," said Newt, "and every Republican has to ask themselves the question, do you really want Harry Reid back as the majority leader?"[2]

Not surprisingly, Newt's presence attracted the media, and the media presence attracted a dozen or so protestors to the luncheon fund-raiser, many of them wearing pink Planned Parenthood T-shirts. The pink, I gathered, was to show their solidarity with women and girls. Did they not, I wondered, see the terrible irony in supporting a worldwide abortion regime that singles out unborn baby girls for termination? In many parts of the world, and even in some parts of America, when a doctor looks at an ultrasound and announces, "It's a girl," he is issuing a death sentence. According to the United Nations, as many as 200 million females have disappeared from the world's population because of gender-specific abortions. Each year, India and China abort more girls than are born in the United States.[3]

These protestors could not have thought through their position carefully. One particularly confused guy from Planned Parenthood was wearing a shirt that read, "I'm a woman and I vote." One woman came to this same event dressed as a birth control pill. Another woman was chanting mindlessly, "You can't escape. It's still called rape. You can't escape. It's still called rape."[4] Escape what? Who said it wasn't called rape? Here we were advancing the nation's highest ideals, and here was our opposition demanding the right to kill off future generations before they were even conceived, a "right" that unfortunately wasn't even under threat. "Let's shut Todd Akin down," the protestors shouted, knowing they had no argument to make that could survive a debate.

The protestor that caused us the most trouble also happened to be the smallest one. It happened this way. We were to shoot our first anti-Claire ad after the Republican Convention. The film crew had unpacked and had set up cameras, lights, and reflectors. The make-up lady had painted my face, and we were ready to start filming on Debbie Cochran's beautiful front porch. The teleprompter started rolling, and I started in something to the effect of, "I misspoke for six seconds, but Sen. Claire McCaskill has voted like Obama for six years!" Before I could finish we heard this annoying sound— Screeeeeeeeeeeechchchchchch!

"Cut!" yelled the director. "The sound track was junk; start over."

It was a cicada, just one. That is all it took. Those who live in the Midwest know I'm not exaggerating—these big insects sound like a rattlesnake on steroids when they get going. We waited a few minutes for him to shut up. When the cicada seemed to catch his breath, we tried again. Really, is thirty seconds of quiet too much to ask?

Screeeeeeeeeeeechchchchchch!

It went on like this for over an hour! We never got a clean thirty seconds.

Finally, Perry realized that extraordinary measures were necessary. He went to the edge of the yard and climbed the medium-sized sweet gum tree about ten feet off the ground and gave the tree a shake. Silence!

We got the camera rolling, then, you guessed it— Screeeeeeeeeeeechchchchchch!

Now things were getting personal for our Marine campaign manager. Perry climbed another ten feet to the point where the branches were getting very small compared to his weight and shook the tree like a tornado. Finally the cicada decided that a strategic retreat was called for. Away he buzzed in a zigzag flight to a far-off tree. Campaign management is hazardous duty. Lights . . . Camera . . . Action!

This was one of the lighter moments in an otherwise intense campaign. Phyllis Schlafly, the grand dame of conservative politics, captured conservative outrage best in an op-ed the day after Rove's "murder" remarks were made public. "Karl Rove has made himself toxic to Republicans by his incredibly offensive and dangerous statement suggesting the murder of Congressman Todd Akin of

Missouri," said Schlafly. "Any candidate or network who hires Rove will now be tarnished with this most malicious remark ever made in Republican politics."[5]

Schlafly also explained why my candidacy troubled Rove, namely my refusal to vote for President George W. Bush's expansion of Medicare. "Akin is a man of principle who doesn't cave in to political pressure," said Schlafly. "So he's not Rove's kind of politician." Schlafly, who is from St. Louis, summed up the sentiments of many Show-Me Staters, "Missourians don't want politicians from other states telling us who to run for the Senate."[6] Phyllis has never been afraid to speak her mind. At eighty-eight, she was still willing to man the ramparts. That is what has made her such a force in our nation's history.

For those too young to remember, Phyllis Stewart earned her undergraduate and master's degrees during World War II while working as a ballistics gunner and technician at a major ammunitions plant. She married John Schlafly after the war, and together they raised six children, a number that resonates in the Akin household. Later, she would earn a law degree from Washington University. Always politically active, in 1972 Schlafly took it upon herself to stop the progress of the potentially disastrous Equal Rights Amendment, an amendment that had already cleared Congress and been ratified by twenty-eight of the necessary thirty-eight states. Her efforts eventually paid off, and the feminist establishment never forgave her. For this and Schlafly's other extraordinary achievements, Ann Coulter calls her one of the "four or five most important men or women of the twentieth century."[7] Schlafly well represented the Show-Me spirit of Missouri women in particular and conservative women in general.

Another woman with patriotic spirit had worked in my district office for the previous twelve years. I had hired Debbie Cochran, a seasoned health care professional, right after I was elected to Congress in 2000. She proved to be an excellent choice. On that very Sunday night, when Debbie saw the heat I was taking as an alleged enemy of women, she took it upon herself to submit a proposal for an all-female entity that would counter that image. She quickly enlisted several women, one of whom was Heather Kesselring, a high-energy home-educating mom we had known since she was a little girl playing volleyball with our kids. In the five days between the Jaco show and the Friday press conference, they had created an impressive organization that would come to be known as Missouri Women Standing with Todd Akin.

Our campaign supported their effort and helped coordinate their activities, but as Perry would attest, these women needed little guidance. They put together a brochure and a video, both of which featured the testimony of a wide range of racially diverse women, young and old. What these women had to say was heartfelt and often moving. In declaring their support of our campaign, they talked about a wide range of issues. "The War on Women is . . . pornography, it is sex trafficking, it is abortion," Heather told a crowd of about two hundred women in St. Louis in mid-September. "And it is time to say, 'Todd Akin understands these issues, and he is ready to go fight for women like nobody else.'"

Sensing an uptick in our poll numbers among women, McCaskill fired back with a series of ads that featured women who had been raped. Predictably, they denounced my comments on the Jaco show as well as my opposition to the so-called morning-after pill, which is essentially a form of abortion. What was troubling about the ads is that two of the women described themselves as "pro-life." Unfortunately, in describing themselves as such, they diluted the meaning of the term. If they lent their reputation to elect a pro-abortion senator who walked in lockstep with the most pro-abortion administration in history, they were clearly not helping the life cause.

As our women's group traveled around the state, they were joined by beautiful people who had an altogether different experience with rape: these young people were the "products" of rape. Many of their mothers had realized the truth about abortion. In their emotional pain, they had recognized the humanity of the child within, and those children had graced their mothers' lives in ways even the mothers could not have anticipated. As you might imagine, these young people believed themselves as deserving of life as those conceived in an act of love. They resent the pressure by even well-meaning friends to push a mother to abort a child conceived in rape.

"As always, mainstream media treats people groups [*sic*] as monolithic without ever bothering to discover what people actually believe and do. They instinctively and gleefully paint pro-life support of children born of rape as 'extreme,' thereby attempting to silence any discussion." The multiracial Ryan Bomberger knows whereof he speaks. He was himself conceived in rape.[8]

Rebecca Kiessling is a beautiful and courageous leader for those good souls across America who were conceived in rape. Her personal story is incredible, and that story and many others are available at www.rebeccakiessling.com. I am deeply grateful for her help in our campaign and for her national leadership.

In its sixty-two action-packed days, Missouri Women Standing with Todd Akin staged eight rallies around the state, three luncheons, and four prayer breakfasts. Some of our local Missouri women gave fabulous, heartfelt testimonies. These talks were as strong as any I had ever heard in politics. The national media did not pay the group much mind, but the local media tended to give its events fair coverage. The McCaskill camp was trying to convince Missouri that all women think alike and that they had no greater concern—if Democrat poster girl Sandra Fluke were to be believed—than easy abortion and free birth control pills. In Missouri at least, Missouri Women Standing with Todd Akin was determined to prove them wrong.

Compounding the difficulty of our mission was that my opponent was a woman, and I was not. This made our debates a little ticklish. On the one hand, the media were insisting that there was so little difference between genders that women were fit to become boxers, firefighters, even combat-ready soldiers. On the other hand, if a male candidate appeared to take too tough a stand against a female candidate in a debate, at least a female Democrat, he might never live it down. Ask Rick Lazio, the Republican who ran against Hillary Clinton for US Senate in 2000. "Many supporters of Mrs. Clinton said they found Mr. Lazio to be pushy and disrespectful during the debate in Buffalo," wrote the *New York Times*, "bullying her in a way that he would not have bullied a male opponent."[9] Given my newly hatched reputation as an enemy of women, I was determined to avoid what pundits still call a "Rick Lazio moment."[10]

To help me prepare for the first debate, which was sponsored by the Missouri Press Association and held in Columbia, we brought in Bill and Bev Randles. Bill had just come off an unsuccessful grassroots campaign in the Republican gubernatorial primary. Although hugely outspent, Bill was never outdebated. We had never seen anyone better. He had picked up some of his skills at Harvard Law School, where Barack Obama had been one of his classmates. Bev, Bill's beautiful and articulate wife, played the role of Claire McCaskill in our debate practices. She was tough.

One thing Bill helped me avoid was my engineer's tendency to jump right into the details. He schooled me to start with the big questions, then move into policy, and finally into details. The preparation paid off. I went first in the Columbia debate and was fresh and ready. For the allotted two minutes, I talked about the "things that matter"—my wife of thirty-seven years, my six children, three of whom served in the Marine Corps, my eight grandchildren, and our great love for this country. That much said, I acknowledged, "Things are not all right." I cited the lack of jobs, the enormous growth of debt, and the intrusion of Washington into our lives. The choice, I argued, was "more freedom or more Washington." I said all of this hopefully and with civility. The trick with a televised debate, especially against a woman, especially given the hysteria about my past remarks, was to be myself and stay likable. This I think we accomplished.

By contrast, Claire came out of the gate nervous and shrill. She talked not at all about her family or our future, but about me. "I'm in the middle," she insisted. "He's so far on the fringe." She talked about how I had worked with "Michelle Bachman," a code word on the far left for "fanatic," but proof for those not in on the code that I work well with women. "I'm proud of my strong moderate record," Claire insisted.

"Claire can say she's a 50 percenter," I said with a smile when given a chance to respond, "but when you vote 98 percent of the time with Obama and then tell us you're a regular middle-of-the-roader, that takes guts."[11] It went back and forth from there. She talked about what an extremist I was. I talked about her voting record. She played prosecutor. I played the conciliator. I can't say for sure that I won, but we were high-fiving afterward, while Claire stormed off yelling at her campaign manager. She also canceled all future debates save for the one that was fixed in granite.

If Missourians knew nothing about the campaign except what they had seen in that debate in Columbia, I would have won in a landslide. But that's not the way debates work at any level, save perhaps for the presidential ones. Few voters watched the debate. More read about the debate as filtered through the media. The Midwest Voices column in the *Kansas City Star*, for instance, was headlined, "McCaskill destroys Akin in debate." The columnist, Yael Abouhalkah, wrote, "She was really trying to portray herself as a moderate on a number of issues, trying to attract independent votes in this hard-fought election. But she's really a liberal on many issues, and that's not really a bad thing."[12] Being a liberal wouldn't be a bad thing in Massachusetts, maybe, but in Missouri—at least outside the *Star* newsroom—it is a losing proposition. Obama lost Missouri in 2008. In 2012, he lost by ten percentage points.

A week later, a reporter was asking me about the debate. In response, I compared McCaskill's demeanor in the recent debate to that which she exhibited in her 2006 race against Jim Talent. Speaking of McCaskill's tone in her 2006 debate, I said, "She had a confidence and was much more ladylike," I told the reporter, "but in the debate on Friday she came out swinging, and I think that's because she feels threatened."[13] Apparently, when I was not paying attention through the years, the word *ladylike* had become an insult. The media, especially the more leftist portions thereof, erupted into another mini-firestorm, and McCaskill sucked up all the airtime she could nursing her wounds in public.

Following our successful debate, we had some ground to recover from the widely respected Missouri Farm Bureau. Soon after the primary, I met with the Bureau members to seek their endorsement. I did not pretend that my repeated votes against the Farm Bill were mistakes. I explained that the bills were freighted with social welfare measures that harmed the country in the long run and that, as long as these measures were in future bills, I would continue to vote against them. I managed to persuade all but two of the two-hundred-plus members who were present to endorse me. After the "legitimate rape" blow-up, the Farm Bureau made the unusual decision to retract their endorsement. At that time, someone quoted Roy Blunt as saying, "What Roy giveth, Roy can take away." This was in the context of the Farm Bureau endorsement. A week or two later, I returned to try to regain their endorsement, and I got it, with an overwhelming majority. These were some of the best people on the planet—straightforward, honest, and patriotic. They understood political pragmatism, but they preferred to vote on principle.

In the weeks that followed the Jaco show, a constant media question was "Is Akin staying in?" I suspect some of my party friends might have circulated some rumors to the contrary, in order to hurt our fund-raising. In fact, I had been carefully considering what was best for everyone. Weighing my alternatives, I realized our war on two fronts was an up-hill battle at best. The Republicans were inflicting considerable damage, and the media were relentless. As I have made clear, however, conservatives also weigh heavily the question, "What is right?"

Along these lines, I recalled that in Missouri, we have a primary election process. The people of Missouri had chosen me by a significant margin. I had been given a solemn charge. They had entrusted me with a job to do. Many people had sacrificed for my victory, and now party leaders were encouraging me to walk away, to cut a deal to somehow feather my own nest? I didn't see it that way. I saw that as betraying a trust. I saw that as giving party bosses the new power to eliminate someone who won his primary and replace that person with their handpicked successor. The primary was an election, not a selection.

Some in the party, and many in the blogosphere, would accuse me of being selfish for staying in the race. I am not sure I understand that line of reasoning. My selfish gene was telling me to get out of the race and go back to building stuff in my workshop. Running for office, especially under these circumstances, was as far from the dictionary definition of "fun" as any activity I could possibly imagine. Plus, by withdrawing I could regain the good graces of many of my colleagues. "We will rally around Akin as GOP hero if he withdraws for the good of the country," said commentator Ann Coulter. "Roe is at stake!"[14] She was not the only one singing that tune.

For all her smarts, Coulter, like many others, did not do her homework. She and the others were laboring under the misconception that a generic Republican could still beat McCaskill. That task would have been difficult under the best of circumstances. After several weeks of this all-out Republican food fight, it would have been impossible. It would first have required the party to select a candidate; second to put a campaign together in two months; and third to raise many millions of dollars in the hope of beating a seasoned incumbent Democrat in a year when no incumbent Democratic senator was to be beaten. To claim that Missouri would have been the only exception goes beyond the speculative to the downright ridiculous.

Thankfully, we were not all alone. There were quite a number of prominent conservatives in addition to Newt Gingrich and Phyllis Schlafly who ignored the hostile fire and stood side by side with me. Presidential candidate Mike Huckabee supported us from the get-go. We even played some country music together in Joplin. I had a sense he understood what it was like to face a hostile media and unsympathetic party bosses. Mike's wife, Janet, also made the

Missouri Women for Standing with Todd Akin trip across the state, and she is no pushover. In addition, Star Parker joined our team. She is a vivacious syndicated columnist, social critic, author, and conservative Republican political activist. She is a former welfare mother who has seen firsthand the damage that a life of dependency renders. We had many other great people support us too. I will never forget their support.

We were also blessed by the support of Oklahoma senator Jim Inhofe, Iowa congressman Steve King, former Oklahoma congressional leader J. C. Watts, Georgia congressman Dr. Phil Gingrich, and Col. Ollie North. These brave souls all did events with us, and some even traveled with us. In addition, a shining cloud of witnesses surrounded us and helped in every imaginable way. These included Jim Bob and Michelle Duggar and their family, our dear friends Dr. Jim and Shirley Dobson of Focus on the Family, Dick and Shirley Bott and their son Rich Bott of the Bott Radio network, fellow home educator Dana Loesch, Dr. Gina Loudon, longtime conservative leader Tony Perkins of the Family Research Council, our good friends David and Cheryl Barton of WallBuilders, and US Atty. Gen. John Ashcroft and his wife, Janet. There were others too. Many of these prominent and visible supporters were from outside the state, yet we were surrounded by regional leaders and very influential stalwart patriots from within the state as well.

These great patriots understood the importance of standing up for what we believe is right. Together, we would stand against both parties and fight our way back.

By staying in the race, I stood against the high-handed tactics of the party bosses and their refusal to support what had always been the party platform. I stood against the media bullies who are outrageously one-sided and who are frequently outright dishonest in their reporting. I stood up to the scorn of a public led to believe lies, and I stood up for the lives of the innocent and the great principles that define the good in America.

I did it not because it was easier, nor to seek the limelight or the title "Senator." I did it for the same reason that I had opposed bad legislation pushed by various power brokers over the previous twenty-four years. I did it because I believed it was the right thing to do. I recalled Winston Churchill's speech at his alma mater, the Harrow School, during World War II: "This is the lesson: never give in, never give in, never, never, never—in nothing, great or small, large or petty—never give in except to convictions of honor and good sense. Never yield to force; never yield to the apparently overwhelming might of the enemy."[15]

I stood, but I did not stand alone. Around me was a great host of wonderful patriots and conservatives. I will never forget their support in our hour of need. God promises us He will never leave us nor forsake us, and He didn't.

# 20

# BACKFIRE

Among those people who condemned my remarks on the Jaco show was Richard Mourdock, the Indiana state treasurer then running for an open Senate seat in Indiana. "Mr. Akin's comments about the heinous crime of rape were callous and offensive," said Mourdock at the time. "I condemn Mr. Akin's remarks, and he needs to make a complete apology for them."[1]

I don't know Mourdock personally, but I was disappointed by his response given that he is a serious pro-lifer and a principled conservative.

In February 2011, Mourdock shocked the go-along, get-along wing of the Republican Party by announcing his candidacy against six-term incumbent Richard Lugar. Lugar, who had not lived in Indiana in the last thirty-six years, was consistently among the five most liberal Republicans in the Senate, and he seemed to be getting more liberal the longer he lived in DC. Then, too, Lugar was eighty at the time of the 2012 election.

As soon as Mourdock announced, establishment Republicans began to grumble. The Republican incumbent, Lugar, was a sure thing. Given his high profile as chairman of the Senate Committee on Foreign Relations, he had a proven ability to raise money. He had won every general election by comfortable margins, so comfortable, in fact, that the Democrats did not put up a candidate to oppose him in 2006.

Mourdock was a relative nobody, a small-town guy and an evangelical Christian. A geologist by training and an entrepreneur, he got his master's degree not at an Ivy League school but at Ball State—a surefire punch line on the *Late Show With David Letterman*. Mourdock was fifty-five when first elected to statewide office, and then upset the business establishment when, as state treasurer, he sued to block the federal bailout of Chrysler. The fact that various Tea Party groups were supporting Mourdock made him all the more suspect.

Despite limited funds, Mourdock was making headway against Lugar. As the June 2012 primary approached, Beltway Republicans grew increasingly anxious. John McCain and Indiana governor Mitch Daniels endorsed Lugar. The American Action Network, a DC-based "center-right" organization tied to the permanent political class, invested nearly $600,000 in anti-Mourdock ads. And a number of big donors put their money into pro-Lugar Super PACs.[2]

Senate seats are expensive. When a relatively safe seat comes open, the candidate who has his hands on the retiring senator's Rolodex has a major leg up on his opponents. Establishment Republicans have considerable power in putting that Rolodex in the right hands. They knew that Lugar was running because he had nothing better to do, and they also understood that Indiana would be inclined to elect a Republican for an open seat, but Mourdock was not the kind of Republican they wanted. He was not their boy. As it turned out, it did not matter what they thought. The combined efforts of the establishment Republicans netted Lugar 39 percent of the vote. Indiana Republicans had apparently decided that Lugar had long since passed his sell-by date.

As the general election campaign headed down the home stretch, Mourdock was well positioned to defeat Democratic congressman Joe Donnelly. Then came the fateful debate on October 23. "I know there are some who disagree, and I respect their point of view, but I believe that life begins at conception," said Mourdock. "I just struggled with it myself for a long time, but I came to realize: life is that gift from God that I think even if life begins in that horrible situation of rape, that it is something that God intended to happen."[3]

By this time, the Democrats and their friends in the media had all the $x$'s and $o$'s mapped out in their Republican "war on women" game plan. "As a pro-life Catholic, I'm stunned and ashamed that Richard Mourdock believes God intended rape," said Dan Parker, the strategically outraged chairman of the Indiana Democratic Party. "Victims of rape are victims of an extremely violent act, and mine is not a violent God. Do we need any more proof that Richard Mourdock is an extremist who's out of touch with Hoosiers?"[4]

I could write an essay deconstructing Dan Parker's phony outburst. Given his declared status as a pro-life Catholic, I wonder how he aligned himself with this particular plank in the Democrat's 2012 platform: "The Democratic Party strongly and unequivocally supports *Roe v. Wade* and a woman's right to make decisions regarding her pregnancy, including a safe and legal abortion, regardless of ability to pay. We oppose any and all efforts to weaken or undermine that right." On the face of it, it seems totally inconsistent to assert one is pro-life and at the same time a Democrat. Those who say they are both, like Dan Parker, often use their alleged pro-life stance to subvert the candidacy of real pro-lifers, just as Dan Parker did.

Of course, this was the same Democratic Party that, in the name of "pro-choice," was denying Dan Parker's Catholic Church any choice. It was a big-government, top-down edict that the Church must become an accomplice with the abortion industry. It must subsidize contraception, sterilization, and abortion-inducing drugs, fully and consciously against its will. And yes, too, this was the same party that cheered as a known sexual predator and credibly accused rapist gave its keynote speech. If someone had the right to be "stunned and ashamed," it was Dan Parker's fellow churchgoers.

Today, if I google "Akin Mourdock," I get 171,000 hits. You

can imagine the couplings. *Slate* titled its article, "The Party of Rape. Every time the GOP claims to have purged rape extremism, another Republican opens his mouth."[5] *US News* headlined its story, "Richard Mourdock's Todd Akin Moment."[6] And finally, two weeks later, there were scores of gloating headlines like this one from the *Hill*, "Abortion-rights groups cheer Akin, Mourdock defeats."[7] Establishment Republicans were reluctant to condemn Mourdock, and some halfheartedly defended him, like Katrina Trinko, whose *NRO* article "Mourdock Isn't Second Akin" tried to split the difference between us.[8]

This was, however, all too little, too late. Instead of attacking the Democrats when they had the chance two months earlier, Republicans validated the Democratic strategy. By this time, the pattern was established. Use the words "rape" and "abortion" in a sentence, and you were toast. "God creates life, and that was my point," said Mourdock in his own defense. "God does not want rape, and by no means was I suggesting that he does. Rape is a horrible thing, and for anyone to twist my words otherwise is absurd and sick."[9] He was right. Those twisting his words in October were absurd and sick, but they were no more absurd and no more sick than those twisting my words in August.

There was a profound issue to be debated here. It spoke directly to who we were as a people, but by running away from it, the Republicans yielded the high ground to the Democrats. This abdication came back to haunt Republican Ken Cuccinelli in the 2013 Virginia governor's race. As Fred Barnes reported in the *Weekly Standard*, Cuccinelli assumed that if he shied from speaking of social issues like abortion, the Democrats would too. They didn't. His opponent, Terry McAuliffe, spent something like $7 million on ads blasting Cuccinelli as "too extreme for Virginia."[10]

Even more pointedly, the McAuliffe campaign sent out an e-mail titled "Virginia's Todd Akin." It read, in part: "It's undeniable: Akin and Cuccinelli are two peas in a pod. They both support Personhood bills that would ban many common forms of birth control, including the pill. While Cuccinelli might be a good enough politician not to say something as abhorrent as 'legitimate rape,' he believes that abortion should be illegal even in the case of rape and incest—just like Todd Akin."[11]

On this subject, lying comes easily to Democrats. Neither Cuccinelli nor I ever talked about banning "the pill" as that term is commonly understood. If the Left felt free to "disinform" the public, the Right blindly misinformed it. The *Weekly Standard* article on the aforementioned e-mail repeated the now common canard that I "claimed pregnancy as a result of rape did not happen." But no one questions this misquote. It has become knee jerk, like my word "legitimate." Can anyone explain why the law enforcement phrase "legitimate rape" is "abhorrent"? *Ambiguous*, yes; *awkward*, perhaps; but *abhorrent*, no. That is pure propaganda—the twisting of words.

Speaking of extremes, McAuliffe endorsed abortion on demand with no exceptions, a position that only 26 percent of Americans support, according to a recent Gallup poll.[12] Unfortunately, almost no one in Virginia knew McAuliffe's position. Cuccinelli did not have the money to expose it, and even if he had, his advisers would have talked him out of it. "Republicans are as clueless as ever in combating the charge they're waging a 'war on women,'" concluded Barnes accurately. "Mitt Romney failed last year to deal with it. He went limp. This year Cuccinelli did the same. He ignored the charge and paid a heavy price. Now Democrats have every reason to continue using the tactic."[13] It will not surprise you to learn that the *Weekly Standard* failed to take the offensive in 2012 against the "war on women" nonsense. In fact, both Barnes and editor William Kristol cheered on those calling for my removal.

In a September 2012 column titled, "Debbie Wasserman Akin," Kristol wondered why the Democrats did not repudiate their national chair, Debbie Wasserman Schulz, for having "doubly lied about a matter of international import" in regard to Israel. By contrast, my remarks were merely "stupid and offensive." Asked Kristol rhetorically, "Will reporters ask leading Democrats whether they stand by their national chair? . . . Will any Democrats have the courage to call on Debbie to go?" The answers, of course, are no and no. And yet here was Kristol, bragging that "GOP leaders announced they were cutting off support for [Akin's] Senate race and launched a concerted effort to persuade him to withdraw."[14] On the Armed Services Committee we might have called the Republican strategy "unilateral disarmament." As history records, it never works.

We Republicans refuse to learn. In January 2014, my friend Mike Huckabee made the perfectly cogent comment at an RNC meeting that Democrats were telling women that "they are helpless without Uncle Sugar coming in and providing for them a prescription each month for birth control because they cannot control their libido or their reproductive system without the help of government." The mention of the word "libido" triggered much fake Democratic outrage and sent apologetic RNC chair Reince Priebus scurrying to the nearest microphone to insist that we Republicans "must all be very conscious of the tone and choice of words we use."[15] Said Whittaker Chambers, who knew whereof he spoke, "The great failing of American conservatives is they do not retrieve their wounded."[16]

This all raises the interesting question—why is it that Republicans are afraid to take a stand? We are the ones who should express righteous indignation at the Democrats' dishonesty, duplicity, and even indifference to murder, in the womb and out. After all, as Hillary memorably declared about the Benghazi killings of our ambassador, information officer, and security operatives, "What difference at this point does it make?"

The problem with the leaders of the Republican Party, I believe, is that they have forgotten who we are. They have forgotten the connection between faith and freedom. They have forgotten the very words of our national anthem—"blest with victory and peace, may the heaven-rescued land / Praise the Power that hath made and preserved us a nation!" In 2012, they stuck to safe subjects, like the mathematics of a broken budget and an unworkable federal takeover of health care and let the Democrats use our silence on moral issues against us. They were afraid it would not be "cool" to talk of the righteous zeal that comes from knowing truth, would not be cool to call abortion what it is—murder—and condemn it, would not even be cool to call socialism what it is, namely, institutionalized theft.

They are practically afraid to acknowledge our Founders' dependence on God, or our own, for that matter. We have watched our great nation falling apart in front of us. It is not too late, however, to shore up our foundation. America is a unique and noble country, with a level of freedom and prosperity that is historically unprecedented and the envy of the world. Those of us who have grown up here need to remind ourselves of our many blessings, ask God's forgiveness, and return to His ways.

Our ascendancy as a nation was never about natural resources. It was always about character. Our founding was marked by courageous people with great dreams. There is the incredible adventure of men, women, and children crossing the rough North Atlantic to start a civilization. In the Mayflower Compact, these free people, under God, created a civil government to frame just and equal laws. God would grant the Puritans who followed, Gov. John Winthrop prophesied, a "shining city on a hill" if only they followed God's law.

The Founders drew on the principles of the Pilgrims' Mayflower Compact in the Declaration of Independence, asserting, "We hold these truths to be self-evident, that all men are . . . endowed by their Creator with certain unalienable Rights, that among these are *Life*, Liberty, and the pursuit of Happiness." Soon after signing the Declaration, Samuel Adams declared, "We have this day restored the Sovereign to Whom all men ought to be obedient. He reigns in heaven and from the rising to the setting sun, let His kingdom come."[17] Nearly a century later, in his last public address, the first Republican president, Abraham Lincoln, reminded the nation that on the eve of peace, "He, from whom all blessings flow, must not be forgotten."[18]

More than 350 years after Winthrop called for this new land to serve as a shining city on a hill, President Ronald Reagan echoed his call in his farewell address of January 1989. "I've spoken of the shining city all my political life, but I don't know if I ever quite communicated what I saw when I said it," said Reagan. "But in my mind it was a tall, proud city built on rocks stronger than oceans, windswept, God-blessed, and teeming with people of all kinds living in harmony and peace."[19]

Our campaign in Missouri used this very same message that has resonated so clearly from Winthrop to Reagan. Our freedom depends on our faith. That is what has made us unique as a nation. If we revive our faith in God and in America, we can restore the America that has been a beacon of hope for oppressed people around the world. We can rebuild the America that has lifted millions out of disease and abject poverty. We can pass on to future generations the most precious gift that can be given—One Nation under God!

# 21

# REVIVAL

A political campaign is not quite as brutal as a military campaign, but there are enough parallels that the word *campaign* works comfortably for both. Like Rev. John Peter Muhlenberg, the Lutheran minister who led his congregation to war in 1776, many pastors throughout Missouri understood that Christians had as much right to the public square as any other citizens. Knowing the leadership role the pastors played in Republican politics, the state party leadership got it into their collective heads to use the clergy to sabotage my campaign. They approached several but succeeded only in alienating Christian activists even more. Thomas Jefferson understood the faith-freedom connection, which I emphasized while campaigning. On his monument in DC it reads in part, "God who gave us life gave us liberty. Can the liberties of a nation be secure when we have removed a conviction that these liberties are the gift of God?"

Jefferson understood that before people will risk their lives and fight for something, they must first understand that their cause is just and right. They must believe in their heart of hearts that their liberty (or freedom) is a gift of God that is being stolen. Therefore, if faith is removed, freedom will soon follow.

More and more, my campaign took on the air of a patriotic revival. Mocked by the media, reviled by the Democrats, shunned by our own party, we traversed the state, in a well-traveled rental car, with high hopes and even higher spirits. My daughter-in-law's incredible brother, Jonathan; our fantastic regional director, Brett Adams, and his wonderful family; and our other regional coordinators had all done yeomen's work spreading yard signs across the state, and we saw them everywhere, many more than we saw for McCaskill. Her campaign message seemed to be, "I'm not Todd Akin," and although that was enough to generate votes, it was not enough to generate the kind of enthusiasm we were experiencing.

I remember several rallies in smaller counties, some at county fairgrounds, some outdoors, some indoors. Some of my speeches recalling who we are as a country resonated in people's hearts. I could almost see a glow emanating from those in attendance, all of them sensing that we were in this together, all Americans, all brothers and sisters, regardless of race or creed or color or age or sex. The campaign was developing a rhythm. Our air support was minimal, but our ground support was strong and getting stronger. As the campaign moved along, the events got bigger, the crowds more intense, and the speeches got more precise. Although I did not know if I was going to win—only God knew that—I at least had the opportunity to reinforce the Founders' sentiments on the role of the Creator in securing our freedom.

"We hold these truths to be self-evident, that all men are created equal, that they are endowed by their Creator with certain unalienable Rights, that among these are Life, Liberty, and the pursuit of Happiness," wrote Thomas Jefferson in our critical and foundational document, the Declaration of Independence. Every talk I gave I reinforced the idea of the Creator, a concept at the heart of our founding documents. Although the role of the Creator was self-evident to me and my supporters, it was not at all self-evident to our opponents. Nor, obviously, was the concept of "life." In our own small way, we were fighting to preserve life and liberty against a party that more and more openly despised the precepts upon which our freedom rested and our future hung.

In the past, I had not been shy about sharing my honest thoughts about the Democratic agenda. In June 2011, I had stirred a good deal of phony outrage when I commented on NBC's decision to remove the words "under God" from the Pledge of Allegiance during its coverage of the US Open. "I think NBC has a long record of being very liberal, and at the heart of liberalism really is a hatred for God and a belief that government should replace God," I told Tony Perkins on his radio program.[1] I spoke here not about individual liberals but about the movement itself, and despite calls for an apology, I would not take back the comment.

At their convention in September 2012, the Democrats showed just how accurate my comment was. Reacting to his party's decision to remove from its platform all mention of God and any reference to Jerusalem as the capital of the State of Israel, Ohio governor Ted Strickland made a motion to change the platform. "I am here to attest and affirm that our faith and belief in God are central to the American story and informs the value we have expressed in our party's platform," said Strickland hopefully. He then asked that the delegates reaffirm the party's belief in God and its recognition of Jerusalem as Israel's capital.

A generation ago, this would have been a no-brainer, but in 2012 the delegates were not at all keen on obliging one of the few God-fearing men in their midst. When Mayor Antonio Villaraigosa of Los Angeles, the head of the Convention, asked for a two-thirds voice vote of affirmation, he did not get close to what he needed on the first try. He tried again and failed again. After failing a third time and sensing the political disaster at hand, Villaraigosa simply declared that the two resolutions had been passed in the "opinion of the chair." The delegates responded to this declaration with a nasty chorus of boos.[2] As far as I could tell, those people weren't booing God's forced inclusion in the platform because they *loved* Him. No, they were scornful and not afraid to show it.

With the Democrats almost removing God from their platform and Villaraigosa's fraudulent denial of that fact, the media should have covered it in great detail, but reporting on this scarcely lasted a news cycle. The media had more important things to focus on, like my "legitimate rape" comment. I know that's the way the game is played, but we, as Americans, are partially complicit because too many of us, in forgetting who we are and where we came from as a nation, have lost the will to fight for what we believe. One thing we can do is refuse to watch "news" programs or channels or subscribe to newspapers that are liberal. This gets rid of many of them and can, in addition, save you some time.

We have not always been like this. I am reminded of the Reverend Jonas Clarke who, at the urging of Samuel Adams and John Hancock, rallied about seventy of his parishioners in April 1775 to resist a powerful British force of fifteen hundred men with little in the way of armament but "a spirit becoming free-born Americans." Resist they did. Seven of their members died, but they helped rout the mighty British and dispatch these professional soldiers back to Boston with a newfound respect for what faith and freedom can do for a people. The spirit of Lexington and Concord, the "spirit becoming free-born Americans," is a spirit we need to revive.

# 22

# SCORCHED EARTH

On March 23, 2010, President Barack Obama signed the so-called Patient Protection and Affordable Care Act into law. On October 1, 2013, more than twelve hundred days later, the aforementioned law, better known as Obamacare, went into effect. In that same amount of time seventy years earlier—before computers, even—the United States was able to mobilize more than 16 million men and women; produce 105,251 tanks, 324,750 aircraft, and 2,382,311 trucks; and build several atom bombs from scratch—a project that in itself would employ more than 130,000 people—and force the unconditional surrender of Germany and Japan.[1] The government succeeded in doing this by unleashing the power of profit and a free market.

In its first twelve hundred days, by doing the opposite, the Obama administration could not even get its lame website to work, and its mouthpieces were busy complaining that they had not had enough time to get the work done. How far we have fallen!

In a June 2010 referendum, 71 percent of Missourians rejected Obamacare. They don't call us the Show-Me State for nothing. Claire McCaskill was not among the 71 percent. "I understand that parts of it are not popular, but I don't think most Missourians understand what's all in it because it hasn't gone into effect yet," McCaskill said in a June 2012 interview. "I think if they give it a chance, they might be surprised how much they like it."[2] By November 2013, McCaskill was lamenting that although the "health care store [was] open, we've locked the front door."[3]

Unfortunately, our election was in November 2012, not November 2013. Although we could and did run against Obamacare, we could run against it only as a philosophical future evil—namely, an usurpation of freedom—and not as the malfunctioning, promise-breaking monstrosity that it has become. The Democrats must have sensed the disaster ahead. Had they really believed in Obamacare's virtues, they would have rolled it out in 2012 and celebrated its wonders. Instead, they dedicated 2012 to promises that they knew would be broken and busied themselves with attacking truth tellers like me as dangerous.

If I had received a dollar for every time Claire McCaskill called me an "extremist," I might never have had to pick up the phone and ask for money. As it happened, on the day I taped the Jaco show and two days before it aired, Claire attempted to tar me on subjects other than rape and abortion in speaking to Missouri reporters. "He wants to privatize, voucherize" Medicare and Social Security, the *St. Louis Beacon* reported her as saying about me. My comments, she insisted, showed that I was "out of touch with so many Missourians who have worked hard all their lives, who have retired, and who believed that Social Security would be there for them, and believe that Medicare would be there for them." The *Beacon* reporter concluded, "McCaskill's point during the conference call was to paint Akin as an 'extremist' on such issues, citing his campaign statements criticizing both programs."[4]

Let's consider the absurdity of this line of attack. McCaskill and her Democratic colleagues had voted for the most radical overhaul of the American health care system ever attempted. So radical was the plan that they could not get a single Republican in the House or

Senate to go along with it. So hastily was the plan executed that no one read the bill before it was voted on. Said House Speaker Nancy Pelosi for the ages, "We have to pass the [health care] bill so that you can find out what's in it." So hurried was its implementation that no element of the plan had even been tested to see if it worked. And yet I was the extremist for recommending incremental reform of Social Security and Medicare. McCaskill seemed to think so. So, unfortunately, did the media. Such was the nature of the Missouri playing field in 2012.

All of this said, there was something I should have seen coming but did not. This was the scorched earth that Republican leaders had left me to defend. McCaskill knew my point of greatest vulnerability and hit us with an ad so lethal that it almost made me rethink who *I* was voting for. Her team had rounded up the conservative chickens, and now their careless slams of our campaign were coming home to roost. The ad begins with a restrained piano solo and white words superimposed on a black screen, "Is Todd Akin fit to serve in the Senate? Mitt Romney doesn't think so." The ad then cuts to a very sober Romney standing next to Paul Ryan and saying, "What he said was indefensible. It was wrong. It was offensive, and he should step out of the race."

The voice-over continues, "And he is not alone." Now the viewer sees a talking head from some local news show say, "Todd Akin is not at that convention, told by his own party to stay home." On the screen next are images of Kit Bond, Roy Blunt, and John Danforth accompanied by the words, "Even Republican senators from Missouri call Todd Akin 'totally unacceptable.'" Now for the real killer, a cut to John McCain saying on screen, "Frankly he would not be welcome by Republicans in the United States Senate," then back to Romney for a repeat of the coup de grace, "It was offensive, and he should step out of the race."

The ad mercifully concludes with an image of Claire in a down jacket talking to a woman in a supermarket parking lot and her voice-over saying, "I'm Claire McCaskill, and I approve this message."[5] If

I were Claire, I would have approved that message too. I would also have sent thank-you notes to the Republicans who made it possible— John Danforth, Roy Blunt, Kit Bond, John McCain, and especially Mitt Romney. Claire also had the money to drive this message home, and we did not have the money to fight back.

As we traveled the state in that last week, we were not watching TV and not aware of the damage that ad would do. The polls meanwhile were encouraging. Public Policy Polling (PPP) ran an extensive statewide poll on the Friday and Saturday before the Tuesday election that had us down from 48 to 44 percent with 6 percent favoring the Libertarian candidate, Jonathan Dine. In the previous two weeks we had narrowed the gap from six points to four points and had reason to be encouraged. "The big x factor in the Missouri Senate race is Jonathan Dine," said PPP president Dean Debnam at the time. "He's pulling a lot of support from people who would otherwise vote Republican. If they stick with him, then McCaskill will win. But if they decide their desire for a GOP-controlled Senate outweighs their disgust with Akin, then Akin will have a chance to pull the upset."[6]

The word "disgust" suggests the PPP was not exactly in our camp, which made the results all the more heartening. This poll, by the way, just about precisely predicted the outcomes in the presidential, gubernatorial, and lieutenant gubernatorial races. It was a serious poll. True, we had to deal with a media that saw nothing wrong with Debnam's comment, and this was mirrored in a 56 percent unfavorable rating. Still, the media vibe was offset, we felt, by the powerful grassroots energy we were experiencing on the stump. To help mobilize the base in the western part of the state, where I was weakest and Claire was strongest, Newt Gingrich flew into Kansas City for a full day of rallies and fund-raising.

When we learned at the last minute that Newt would be available for breakfast that day, one of our friends arranged to have him speak at a local business-oriented, all-male breakfast club, instead of the local fellow who had been scheduled to speak. As our friend waited outside for Newt to arrive, club members would ask him who was speaking that morning, and he would say, "Newt Gingrich," and they inevitably answered, "No, seriously, who's speaking?" He was being serious.

These were prosperous urban businessmen. Although largely Republican, they represented our hardest sell, with the likely exception of their wives. Upon arriving, Newt asked what he should speak about. We suggested that he speak about something of interest to Missouri businessmen and only pitch my campaign at the end. That is all the direction Newt needed. He held the audience spellbound for an hour on the wonders of fracking and horizontal drilling. More important, he showed the audience that smart, sophisticated Republicans were supporting Todd Akin without apology, and they could do the same. Throughout the day, we were all impressed with just how open and accessible and obliging Newt was.

It happens all the time; I know that candidates feed off the energy around them and come to believe that everyone feels the fire that their supporters do, but we were not foolish in our optimism. We had approached Election Day for the August primary hoping we could come from behind but knowing the outcome was ultimately in God's hands, and we prevailed. In the general election, we again hoped we could come from behind and thought, God willing, we just might. The party apparently thought so too. In the last few days, working through the National Republican Senatorial Conservative Committee, they sent us some funds to save face—just in case.

The weekend before the election, Larry Flynt, the founder of *Hustler* magazine, ran a half-page ad against us in the *St. Louis Post Dispatch*.[7] The media hardly acknowledged it. Apparently, someone who makes money by depicting women as sex objects is not waging a "war on women." But clearly I was. McCaskill was certainly aware of this ad but did not reject support from the pornography industry. Nor did the media ever ask her about it.

Going into Election Day, I had prepared just one speech for that night, with an easy modification for a win or a loss. Early on that evening, I started adjusting it for a loss. Even before the big-city votes returned, the numbers out of the counties we should have been dominating were discouraging. While our people chattered enthusiastically in the ballroom upstairs at the Doubletree, we mulled over the inevitable downstairs. By the time Perry arrived, the green room had all the joy of a morgue, and he did not even have to ask. The news seeped upstairs quickly and quieted the crowd. By eight o'clock we knew we had lost, and by a substantial margin. I did not hesitate to call Claire McCaskill. "You could at least have made the evening more dramatic," I joked, but inside I was hurting. Counting primaries, this was my sixteenth election night party, and it was the first time I had to concede a race. Claire was gracious in victory. I did not expect any different. In person, certainly, she had always treated me with respect.

However, I have long understood something. The media, as one-sided as it is, does not determine our destiny. With Lulli beside me and the children around me, I made this clear in my concession speech right after acknowledging defeat. "It's . . . appropriate to thank God," I said, "who makes no mistakes and is much wiser than we are. To God alone be the honor and the glory—regardless of how He decides to organize history."

I closed my two-minute concession speech the same way I would have closed a victory speech: "As long as we have the courage to stand for what's right and what's good—even when it's very difficult to do—this republic will continue to bring hope to the world and truly be that shining city on the hill. God bless you. God bless America. Good night."

To get a sense of just how far America has strayed off course, consider that USA Today thought my remarks unusual enough to headline its article on my defeat, "Todd Akin references God in concession speech."[8] More telling still, World News headlined its video presentation, "God Makes No Mistakes: Todd Akin's Outrageous Concession Speech."[9] Outrageous? It must have appeared so to people who'd voted to approve gay marriage in four states that very day and reelected as president a would-be socialist who lies as casually as you and I butter our bread. It was not I who said, "There is a just God who presides over the destinies of nations; and who will raise up friends to fight our battles for us." That was Patrick Henry in 1775. Was that outrageous? Without our faith that God is wiser than we are, that November election night would have led to months of total despair. Thank God, literally, it did not.

If there was a silver lining that Election Day, it was that Mitt Romney carried Missouri by nearly ten percentage points. McCain had carried the state by less than one in 2008. In Indiana, Mourdock's remarks obviously did not hurt Romney either. He carried a state that Obama won in 2008 by more than ten points. Our aggressive pro-life stands did not hurt the Republican "brand." On the other hand, the unwillingness of Republican leadership to vigorously defend our party platform could well have cost the party a number of Senate seats.

In fact, Democrats held on to five of their six most vulnerable seats. Not a single Democratic incumbent senator lost reelection. Of the ten races that were considered toss-ups, Democrats won nine. I felt bad for Karl Rove. I had lost one race; he had lost nine. Party leaders could blame the loss of Missouri on me if they liked, but they have to look within to see why they performed so badly across the board, especially considering that Mitt Romney did better against Obama than McCain in every state but two—Alaska because Sarah Palin wasn't in the race and New Jersey because of Hurricane Sandy.

Those winning Democratic senators were riding no wave. In a generally fair-minded article for the *National Journal*, political handicapper Charlie Cook chose not to blame the National Republican Senatorial Committee for the poor performance but rather "a recalcitrant and inflexible base." As Cook saw it, the base was to be faulted because it did not "allow the party to anoint the strongest candidate in a race" the way the Democrats do.[10] Unfortunately, people who think like Cook dominate the leadership of both parties. Perhaps they think we should get rid of primary elections altogether.

There is a case to be made for the repeal of the Seventeenth

Amendment, the one that allows for the direct election of US senators by the people of a state. That I concede. As long as this progressive amendment remains the law, however, it strikes me as more than a little hypocritical that Democrats like Cook would celebrate the exclusion of the citizenry from the electoral process. Besides, Cook missed the point. The problem wasn't that the Republican base chose the candidates. The problem was that the leadership didn't support the choices the base made.

As all losing candidates know, the loss was painful on a more personal level. God had brought together a top-flight campaign team, and I had come to love and respect everyone on the team. We discovered within days that, due to a software misinterpretation, we finished the campaign not $250,000 in the black, as we had assumed, but $250,000 in the red. This meant no severance packages for our loyal staff and a hard fund-raising slog for me. I had never left a campaign in debt before, and I wasn't about to abandon our vendors even if it took a year or more to raise the money we owed.

The one thing that carries us through is our faith. At age sixty-five in November 2012, I had no job as of that January and a mountain of debt. Since then, however, I have had no trouble reminding myself how much I have to be thankful for. I have a wife who loves me. I have two healthy parents who supported me all the way. I have a son who gave up a handsome salary and moved his growing brood to a rental house to manage my campaign, and Perry, of course, was just one of six wonderful children and their several spouses who are still all proud of their father.

In loss, as in my twelve previous victories, I still stand for what I know to be true, right, and good. The winning and losing are in God's hands. I know I have a God who loves me in spite of all my faults. I know He has a plan, and I look forward to the adventure that each new day offers. Thank You, Lord!

# CONCLUSION
# A TIME FOR HEROES

America is a unique country. Nowhere else has a government allowed its citizens the level of freedom, peace, and prosperity that we enjoy. Yes, we have our warts and blemishes, but the fact remains that humanity in general is voting with their feet. We have border fences to keep people out, while some other lands have barbed wire, machine guns, and mines to keep people in.

Do you recall the story about Thomas Schuman, the ex-KGB agent? At the end of his long, terrifying talk I asked the first question: "Thomas, how do you fight these bad ideas?" He answered simply, "Fight bad ideas with the good ideas of America's founding."

We live in a great country because those people who established America understood key principles and put them into our founding documents.

For instance, the Declaration of Independence clearly puts forth the good idea that the purpose of civil government is to protect our natural God-given rights to life, liberty, and the pursuit of happiness. These authors believed that God created each of us in a special way and gifted us so that we could accomplish the unique work that He made just for us. First of all, we could not accomplish our purpose if we were dead; therefore, civil government must protect life. Thus our government was to administer justice so that people could live in harmony and be free to follow their dreams.

Over time, America became known as a land where dreams can become reality. We came to call it the "American Dream." Courageous souls immigrated legally with only the shirts on their backs. They were willing to work hard to provide their families with freedom and a future that they themselves had never enjoyed. Generation after generation, America was built one dream at a time.

Over twenty-four years in elected office I have had the opportunity to talk to groups of Americans. I have frequently asked, "When you boil America down, what is the essence of our country?" Almost always I get one word in response, "freedom."

Unfortunately, too many Americans have not stopped to understand the true meaning of freedom. Freedom does not start in DC. It is not the product of a democratic voting process; far too many despots and tyrants have been elected for that to be true. Nor is freedom the excuse to do anything you want. Freedom is not killing, stealing, and exploiting other people—that is anarchy. True freedom has boundaries. The boundaries are defined by law. God's laws define how freedom works and how one person's freedom is in harmony with someone else's.

Laws were set up when God created the world. One of those laws is the law of gravity. If the US Congress passed a law repealing the law of gravity, you still would not choose to leap from a tall building with a single bound. You might not like the law of gravity, or some other of God's laws, but breaking such a law has consequences. Freedom always involves choices, but you can't separate the choices from the consequences. Don't go jumping off high buildings—it is a bad choice.

I make this obvious example because the Democrat Party has for some years successfully sold the lie that you can do what you want without consequences. Their 2012 platform runs something like this:

- the taking of innocent human lives

- liberal indoctrination in government schools

- government-run health care

- the confiscation of firearms

- onerous government control of businesses

- a Socialistic redistribution of others' wealth

- a barely concealed hostility toward God

This platform shares many tenets of the most ruthless evil totalitarian regimes of the past century. Together, the regimes butchered well over 100 million of their own innocent citizens. Some of these were countries against which our Fathers fought wars both hot and cold.

As incredible as it seems, in 2012 more than 50 percent of American voters bought the lie that you can do what you want without bad consequences. For many of them the logic was simple— someone else has it; you wish you had it; Obama will steal it for you; vote Democratic. The voters chose freebies over freedom. In the process of voting for Democrats and the Democratic platform, they inadvertently chose to be accomplices to murder and stealing. But it was a lie because, as surely as night follows day, bad choices have bad consequences. By choosing freebies they took another step in the destruction of our country and our freedoms.

The Republican leadership was also complicit because they lacked the courage to call evil, EVIL. They made a public spectacle of themselves by fearing to engage the great ethical and moral issues of the day. They lacked the courage to advocate a better way, the American way. They should have spoken of the unsearchable riches of living a life for others, of enjoying a close loving family, of lifting up others with charity, and the excitement that comes from reaching for your dream.

The evil Democratic platform and the spineless Republican leadership alone should be a cause for great alarm; unfortunately, there are many other indicators that likewise testify that America is in serious trouble. Perhaps you sense the danger hanging over America but wonder what we as individual citizens can do about it. We can do a whole lot more than we think we can.

Our problem is not limited to civil government. In previous chapters I have spoken of the fact that self, family, and church governments strongly influence the nature of the civil government. If our citizens were mostly conservatives, our current civil government would look a lot different. Consequently, there are many things that a patriot can do outside of civil government to promote the truth and counter lies.

True freedom builds from the bottom up, and it starts with our "selves." In early America, when people heard the word *government*, they would first think of how each of us, led by God's Spirit, manages his or her own life. They called it "self-government." They understood that the character of a citizen was critical to the nature of the country. A nation peopled by wise, hardworking, loving citizens would be altogether different from a nation of dishonest, self-seeking rogues.

As I recounted earlier, my own experience with self-government began with prayerfully telling Jesus that I was sorry for my sins and asking His forgiveness. I also committed that God would be my Father, and I would try to be obedient to Him. This is the most important decision in anyone's life. It transcends all else, and it is the key to our freedom. When we choose Him, although still tempted by the desires of this world, we are now assisted to choose self-restraint. Even better we have His Spirit to watch over us and guide us in His plan from adventure to adventure.

With some imagination and humor, we can find interesting ways to stand for truth and oppose lies. I mentioned earlier in this book the incident when I ordered the hamburger without onions (page 36). Opportunities are all around us.

While I was a congressman, one of my daughters and I had to wait at the bus station, on Route 6, just outside Hyannis, Cape Cod. The bus was due in about half an hour. Although the state of Massachusetts was supposed to be "green" and "environmentally friendly," the memo somehow never made it to the bus depot. It was thoroughly trashed with soft-drink containers and fast-food packaging. My daughter and I started cleaning it up. We were done in about fifteen minutes and filled several trash barrels. A good number of people saw us, but we didn't say anything, didn't judge anyone, and kept our cheerful demeanor.

What's the point? We had just preached a wordless sermon about cleanliness, and charitable public service and had given an example of self-government. There are lots of ways you can be a freedom fighter.

One of the biggest obstacles to freedom in our country is the power of the national media. As self-governed individuals, however, we have the ability to reduce the power of these media elite. We can choose to boycott their toxic products. The news media would try to convince us that they have the last word on everything current. Much of this is a scam designed to manipulate what people think. In this book, I have exposed how this biased media twists words, creates outrage, and reproduces lies. By turning off the TV and selecting other sources of news, we reduce the liberals' influence.

Everywhere, freedom's enemies are busy twisting word meanings and attempting to force their opinions on others through what is known as "political correctness." We should resist this tactic by defending the truth and each other, especially those on our own team. We need to defend truth especially in those areas where liberals are attacking.

One major front of attack is the desire to publicly deny God, as was evident at the Democrat National Convention. When I served as chairman of the US House SeaPower and Expeditionary Forces Committee, I saw the opportunity to resist their relentless effort to drive God from the public square. I did this by routinely opening our hearings with a prayer to ask God's blessing on all deliberations. I don't know if any other committees opened in prayer or not, but we did, and most people liked it. Eventually the media started asking questions. I told them, "If it is good for Congress to start with prayer, I decided that it would be good to ask God for His blessing on this important work." Today, each of us has the power to introduce prayer in our own domains, even if just a grace before meals at a restaurant.

We can fight politically correct bullying when we condemn evil for what it is. Do you remember the media howls when Reagan rightly called the Soviet Union "the Evil Empire"? When George Bush referred to North Korea, Iraq, and Iran as "the axis of evil," they lost it again. Bullying is best met head-on. When things are bad or evil, speak up.

Aside from confronting bad ideas, self-government calls us to confront our own fears. We must be willing to accept the new challenges God offers us with a cheerful heart. Living this way takes courage because sooner or later, if we keep our hearts open, God will lead us to do the one thing we would most like to accomplish. It is easy to be afraid. No one wants to pursue a dream and fail. We must remember, however, that America was built by courageous people, one dream at a time. Nothing stops us from joining the ranks of freedom fighters, and the best place to start is right where we are. The best time is now.

One of our biggest spheres of influence is our own family. We should be having children, training them to be responsible, and helping them to build strong marriages. Unfortunately, bad ideas are attacking American families.

The Western world has bought the liberal notion that humans are overpopulating planet Earth and destroying it through overproduction and consumption. The "population bomb" was just one of many apocalyptic schemes that liberals hatched to manipulate the masses, "climate change" being only the most recent. One result of this propaganda has been the pursuit of "lifestyle" over life or having children. This pursuit has led to the collapse of the family in Europe and Japan and the impending collapse of their social welfare states because there are not enough young people to sustain their civilizations.

King Solomon wrote in the Bible that children are a blessing from the Lord. As a father of six and grandfather of eleven, I can personally testify to the joy of a big, happy family. My children are best friends with each other, and when we get together for the holidays, or vacation together, the experience is always joyful and enriching. Yes, we might have sacrificed some of the "comforts" that we may have been able to afford with fewer children, but it doesn't seem a sacrifice at all compared to the infinitely better reward of the close family we now have.

One of the biggest sources for the spread of bad ideas is our educational system. For this reason, one mistake conservatives can make is to turn their children over to the government for education. In too many school districts, the education is inferior and the kids are inundated with destructive ideas. In many cases, even with "good" schools, the parents miss the blessing of building a close, loving family. By home educating, we can break the liberal stronghold on education. The high level of adult interaction with their children can help in character development. Building virtuous character is one of the top priorities of most home-educating parents. They typically place a high value on integrity, hard work, cheerful attitudes, obedience, compassion, and self-control.

Another area where bad ideas have wreaked terrible damage has been marriage. Not all broken relationships could be solved by curbed sexual appetite, but there would be a great reduction of divorce and out-of-wedlock births if people could govern themselves. In 1900, America had only half of 1 percent divorce rate; now, nearly half of all American children have experienced the effects of divorce. The cost to the government is enormous, the cost to parents devastating, and the cost to children tragic. It hasn't always been this way and does not have to be this way in the future. Families would do well to lay the groundwork for strong marriages. A significant reduction in the divorce rates and out-of-wedlock births would remedy many of America's social problems and save so many tax dollars that even Libertarians would embrace intentional dating.

Consequently, there are increasing numbers of parents who emphasize purity and "intentional dating" as opposed to recreational dating, a phenomenon that is only a century old. Intentional dating teaches young people not to give their hearts to another until both parties are ready to be responsible parents. In addition, the young man is honest about his intentions to the young lady and gets a green light from parents or guardians before proceeding. Young people are encouraged to develop strong friendships as a foundation of a strong marriage. This was the common road to marriage up to the 1920s.

Perhaps one of the greatest opportunities to return to good ideas and refute bad ideas is through the church. Churches exist in part to warn people of the bad consequences of bad ideas and teach obedience to God's laws. The source of the Founders' good ideas was the Bible. They saw the beautiful harmony between God's Word and the natural world around them. Today, for all the good work our pastors do, many make the mistake of not applying the Bible to the critical issues of our day. This is probably one of the most urgently needed changes in America.

I preface my comments by acknowledging that pastors have the hardest job in the world. It took 50 percent of voters to remove me from office. By contrast, 20 percent of a church membership can oust a pastor.

If we were to ask evangelical pastors, almost all would agree that the Bible contains the principles that should guide us as we live our lives, raise our families, and build our civilization. The problem is that although most evangelicals would say this, many really don't seem to believe it, as witnessed by the churches' silence on the destructive social issues that are savaging the lives of their members.

I believe that if America's pastors do not deal with the application of the Bible to the great questions of our day, it will be too late, and we will never be able to go back. I fear that America's churches will be as empty as most European churches are because people see them as irrelevant (see *Already Gone* by Ken Ham). Otherwise, churches in America will become like those described by Dietrich Bonhoeffer in Germany—churchgoers singing more loudly as the trains of victims roll by.

At the time of our founding, many colonial Puritan sermons were subject sermons. And why not? Pastors were the best educated of citizens and took the lead on the issues of the day. The pastors in America were so involved in the War for Independence that the British quipped, "Cousin America has run off with a Presbyterian parson."

In the 1830s, Alexis de Tocqueville is said to have written, "It wasn't until I came to America's pulpits, aflame with righteousness, that I understood the secret of America's greatness."[1]

Are our pulpits aflame with righteousness? Church members can do several constructive things to make sure they are. First, go to the D. James Kennedy website, http://www.djameskennedy.com/, and download some sermons to see how he dealt with issues. For example, check out "The Bible and Socialism." Second, we can provide support for our pastors by asking them to preach on critical topics. Finally, we can research some topics on our own and teach them in a Sunday school class or use the Truth Project (http://www.thetruthproject.org/) as a curriculum in our churches. What we cannot do . . . is nothing.

In conclusion now, these are the choices before us.

On the one hand, we can choose life and freedom, freedom to live in wonder and amazement at all of the beauties, joys, and deep satisfactions that life offers to those bold enough to dare to travel freedom's road.

On the other hand, we are offered "security," underwritten by the government. We can have the security that we will never fail financially and that our health care, food, and housing will be provided only because the government taxes others to provide it. With government protecting us and feeding us, we won't need to protect ourselves. So the government will take our guns as well. We can have the security to have sex any way we want—the government will provide our birth control, our abortions, and medicine for the STDs we contract along the way. The government that promises us sex without consequences is really selling us a life of broken relationships and loneliness, if not disease and death.

The government will regulate the environment down to the kind of toilets we use and regulate the economy down to the prices we can charge and the wages we can pay. Any other problem that comes up, we can be sure that big government has a plan to make it all okay—much as it is now doing with our health care system. We will be protected by a government whose agents tell us: "You won't have to travel down that dangerous road of freedom, where sorrows lurk around every curve and failure awaits you at road's end."

Before we sign the contract by casting our vote for dependency, we should, of course, read the fine print on the security's contract. It is impossible to separate actions from their natural consequences. If we are guaranteed not to fail, we are guaranteed not to succeed. There can be no great success if there is no risk.

The government that promises to meet our needs, strips us of the dignity and satisfaction of productive labor, and if we work in spite of the disincentives, it will strip us of our wealth to pay for those who don't work.

The government that takes our guns and promises peace will also take our ability to defend our families and our homeland—that didn't work so well for the more than one hundred million who were murdered by their own governments. The man who fails to defend his family and denies his obligation to defend his country is less than a man. If our rights are God-given, should we lightly give up the means to protect those rights?

Before you forsake the crisp air and bright light on the high road of freedom, look well at the velvet-padded chains of government dependency. Although the government chains are well padded, they are chains nonetheless. They threaten to hold America's soul in the gloom, where vision is lost, where monotony and cynicism rule, and where the fresh air and bright sunlight of freedom are only a memory.

We must choose. Remember freedom starts when we choose to do what is right. This is now our battle, and all that is beautiful, good, and true is at stake. You may not be someone important in the eyes of the world, but God delights to use the small people of the world to do great things. Ask Him to forgive you and use you. Ask for a passion in your bones that you can have a focused intensity and a bold determination to be a champion for truth.

This is the time for heroes, but as in the past we do not fight alone. We advance a just cause, serve at the pleasure of God our Father and Creator, and are cheered on by a host of silent witnesses. As for me and my house, we will serve our God and our country.

It has always been the American way to dare greatly, to overcome obstacles, to try and try again, to choose life over fear. And now is the time when the American Dream must rise afresh in brave hearts that have the faith to hope against all odds. Our voices will together swell in chorus, and eyes will moisten and hands will go over hearts, and we will once again sing, "Oh, say can you see . . ." And our children will inherit a land built one dream at a time, and they will stop in childlike wonder and deep thankfulness that they likewise inherited a nation where dreams can still come true.

# NOTES

## CHAPTER 1. THE SILENCE BEFORE THE STORM

1. David Catanese and Alex Isenstadt, "Missouri GOP Senate Primary: McCaskill gets her opponent, Akin wins," *Politico*, August 7, 2012, http://www.politico.com/news/stories/0812/79467.html.

2. Aaron Blake, "Rep. Todd Akin wins primary to face McCaskill in Missouri," *The Washington Post*, August 7, 2012, http://www.washingtonpost.com/blogs/the-fix/post/rep-todd-akin-wins-primary-to-face-mccaskill-in-missouri/2012/08/07/0bce88b6-e0f0-11e1-8fc5-a7dcf1fc161d_blog.html.

3. Associated Press, "Reid's Angle: Attack GOP Foe Angle in Senate Bid," June 16, 2010, http://www.foxnews.com/politics/2010/06/16/reids-angle-attack-gop-foe-angle-senate-bid.

4. "Akin says federal government shouldn't pay for school lunches," *St. Louis Post-Dispatch*, August 16, 2012, http://www.stltoday.com/news/local/state-and-regional/akin-says-federal-government-shouldnt-pay-for-school-lunches/article_42fea0d0-e7a5-11e1-9a61-0019bb30f31a.html.

5. "Editorial: Akin tries to turn back *Post-Dispatch*, August 19, 2012, http://www.stltoday.com/news/opinion/columns/the-platform/editorial-akin-tries-to-turn-back-the-clock-on-child/article_abd42d9d-558b-5c79-8877-6ef50d83edbc.html.

6. Andrew Malcolm, "Barack Obama wants to be president of these 57 United States," *Los Angeles Times*, May 9, 2008, http://latimesblogs.latimes.com/washington/2008/05/barack-obama-wa.html.

7. Jennifer Hoar, "Biden's Comments Ruffle Feathers," CBS News/AP, July 7, 2006, http://www.cbsnews.com/news/bidens-comments-ruffle-feathers.

8.  Mark Preston, "Reid apologizes for 'Negro dialect' comment," CNN Politics, January 9, 2010. http://politicalticker.blogs.cnn.com/2010/01/09/reid-apology-for-negro-dialect-comment.

9.  See "Dan Quayle's 'Potatoe' Incident – 1992," *The Washington Post*, at http://www.washingtonpost.com/wp-srv/politics/special/clinton/frenzy/quayle3.html.

## CHAPTER 2. DEFCON 1

1.  Charles Jaco, "Jaco Report: Full Interview With Todd Akin," Fox2Now video, August 19, 2012, http://fox2now.com/2012/08/19/the-jaco-report-august-19-2012.

2.  Linda Greenhouse, "Supreme Court Rejects Death Penalty for Child Rape," *The New York Times*, June 26, 2008, http://www.nytimes.com/2008/06/26/washington/26scotuscnd.html?pagewanted=all&_r=0.

3.  Cliff Kincaid, "Soros-Funded PAC Started Akin Controversy," NewsWithViews.com, September 4, 2012, http://www.newswithviews.com/Kincaid/cliff643.htm.

4.  John Eligon and Michael Schwirtz, "Senate Candidate Provokes Ire With 'Legitimate Rape' Comment," *The New York Times*, August 19, 2012, http://www.nytimes.com/2012/08/20/us/politics/todd-akin-provokes-ire-with-legitimate-rape-comment.html.

5.  Patrick Buchanan, "A Grand Old Party in Panic," cnsnews.com, August 24, 2012, http://cnsnews.com/blog/patrick-j-buchanan/grand-old-party-panic.

6.  Saul Alinsky, "Saul Alinsky's 12 Rules for Radicals," posted on *Best of Beck* (blog), http://www.bestofbeck.com/wp/activism/saul-alinskys-12-rules-for-radicals.

## CHAPTER 3. STIRRINGS

1.  From Ralph Waldo Emerson's "Concord Hymn," written in 1837 and sung on the Fourth of July at the completion of the Concord Monument.

2.  John Adams, "Message from John Adams to the Officers of the First Brigade of the Third Division of the Militia of Massachusetts," October 11, 1798, posted on beliefnet.com, http://www.beliefnet.com/resourcelib/docs/115/Message_from_John_Adams_to_the_Officers_of_the_First_Brigade_1.html.

3.  Noah Webster, *American Dictionary of the English Language*, 1828, quoted on The Foundation for American Christian Education, http://www.face.net/?page=1828_dictionary.

4.  Edmund Burke, "Letter to a Member of the National Assembly of France," 1791, posted on Wikipedia, January 22, 2012, http://en.wikipedia.org/wiki/Portal:Conservatism/Selected_quote/11.

5.  John Adams, "John Adams' Diary," February 22, 1756, posted on constitution.org, http://www.constitution.org/primarysources/adamsdiary.html.

6. Although this is Edmund Burke's most quoted remark, its provenance is uncertain. http://en.wikiquote.org/wiki/Edmund_Burke.

## CHAPTER 4. AWAKENING: 1985

1. "The Words of the Reverend Schuman," notes from the lecture by Thomas Schuman at the News Word International correspondent's seminar, February 22–24, 1979(?), posted on Tparents.org, http://www.tparents.org/Library/Unification/Talks/Schuman/Schuman-Subvert.html.

## CHAPTER 5. GETTING POLITICAL: 1988

1. John Morton Bloom, *Roosevelt and Morgenthau* (Boston: Houghton Mifflin Harcourt, 1970), 256.

2. Don Phares, "Casino Gaming in Missouri: The Spending Displacement Effect and Gaming's Net Economic Impact," presented at the 2001 Missouri Economics Conference, May 4, 2001, 18.

## CHAPTER 6. GOING TO WASHINGTON: 2000

1. Rick Montgomery, "Republican Senate candidate Todd Akin sticks to his principles," *The Kansas City Star*, October 20, 2012, http://www.kansascity.com/2012/10/20/3876914/akin-sticks-to-his-principles.html.

2. Michael Weisskopf, "Energized by Pulpit or Passion, the Public is Calling: 'Gospel Grapevine' Displays Strength in Controversy over Military Gay Ban," *The Washington Post*, February 1, 1993.

## CHAPTER 7. STATE OF THE UNION: 2001

1. George Washington in his Farewell Address on September 17, 1796, posted at [Federer, William J., *America's God and Country: Encyclopedia of Quotations*, Fame Publishing, Coppell, TX, 1994: 660–661, 828.], http://www.crossroad.to/text/articles/WashingtonFarewell.html.

2. Thomas Jefferson, "And can the liberties of a nation be thought secure when we have removed their only firm basis . . ." *Notes on the State of Virginia*, 1781, posted on Founders' Quotes, http://foundersquotes.com/quotes/and-can-the-liberties-of-a-nation-be-thought-secure-when-we-have-removed-their-only-firm-basis.

3. Jedediah Morse sermon quoted by Dave Miller, "Our Republic Depends on Christianity?" Apologetics Press, https://www.apologeticspress.org/apcontent.aspx?category=7&article=2195.

## CHAPTER 8. SEPTEMBER 11, 2001

1.  Rebecca Solnit, "9/11 showed us who we can be," *Los Angeles Times,* September 11, 2009, http://articles.latimes.com/2009/sep/11/opinion/oe-solnit11.

2.  eMediaMillWorks, "Text: President Bush Addresses the Nation," *The Washington Post,* September 20, 2001, http://www.washingtonpost.com/wp-srv/nation/specials/attacked/transcripts/bushaddress_092001.html.


## CHAPTER 9. TOUGH DECISIONS

1.  "Bush signs landmark Medicare bill into law," CNN.com, December 8, 2003, http://www.cnn.com/2003/ALLPOLITICS/12/08/elec04.medicare.


## CHAPTER 10. GOING TO WAR

1.  Joint Resolution, Pub. L. No. 107–40, 115 Stat. 224 (2001), http://www.gpo.gov/fdsys/pkg/PLAW-107publ40/pdf/PLAW-107publ40.pdf.

2.  Gerard Gawalt, "America and the Barbary Pirates: An International Battle Against an Unconventional Foe," the Thomas Jefferson Papers, the Library of Congress, http://memory.loc.gov/ammem/collections/jefferson_papers/mtjprece.html.

3.  R. W. Apple Jr., "A Military Quagmire Remembered: Afghanistan as Vietnam," *The New York Times,* October 31, 2001, http://www.nytimes.com/2001/10/31/world/nation-challenged-analysis-military-quagmire-remembered-afghanistan-vietnam.html.

4.  Maureen Dowd, "Can Bush Bushkazi?" *The New York Times*, October 28, 2001, http://www.nytimes.com/2001/10/28/opinion/28DOWD.html.

5.  John Kerry, speech at Georgetown University, January 23, 2003, posted on *The Who Said It Game – Iraq Style* (blog), http://www.whosaiditiraq.blogspot.com.

6.  Howard Dean, speech at the California State Democratic Convention, March 15, 2003.

7.  John Cochran, "Kerry Apologizes as 'Stuck in Iraq' Firestorm Rages," ABC News, November 1, 2006, http://abcnews.go.com/Politics/story?id=2621654.

8.  "'Worst' historically-challenged congressman," NBC News video, February 19, 2010, http://www.nbcnews.com/video/countdown/17232707#17232707.

9.  As quoted in Ray Hartmann, "Think Again: Be Still My Akin Heart," *St. Louis*, May 2010, http://www.stlmag.com/St-Louis-Magazine/May-2010/Think-Again-Be-Still-My-Akin-Heart.

10. Associated Press, "Rep. Skelton To Rep. Akin: 'Stick It Up Your Ass,'" *Huffington Post* video, March 18, 2010, http://www.huffingtonpost.com/2009/10/09/rep-skelton-to-rep-akins_n_315821.html.

## CHAPTER 11. THE AGE OF OBAMA

1.   John Avlon, "Obama's steady centrism," *Politico,* July 19, 2008, http://www.politico.com/news/stories/0708/11880.html.

2.   David Brooks, "Run, Barack, Run," The Opinion Pages, *The New York Times,* October 19, 2006, http://www.nytimes.com/2006/10/19/opinion/19brooks.html.

3.   Peggy Noonan, "Obama and the Runaway Train," *The Wall Street Journal,* October 31, 2008, http://online.wsj.com/news/articles/SB122539802263585317?mg=reno64-wsj&url=http%3A%2F%2Fonline.wsj.com%2Farticle%2FSB122539802263585317.html.

4.   Rush Limbaugh, "How in the World Did Dr. Krauthammer and George Will Misjudge Barack Obama?" *The Rush Limbaugh Show,* October 28, 2013, http://www.rushlimbaugh.com/daily/2013/10/28/how_in_the_world_did_dr_krauthammer_and_george_will_misjudge_barack_obama.

5.   Amy Bingham, "'Etch A Sketch' Latest Gaffe From Romney Campaign," ABC News, March 21, 2012, http://abcnews.go.com/Politics/OTUS/etch-sketch-latest-gaffe-romney-campaign/story?id=15973099.

6.   Hart Research Associates, NBC News/Wall Street Journal Survey, July 17–21, 2013, http://msnbcmedia.msn.com/i/MSNBC/Sections/A_Politics/_Today_Stories_Teases/130724-July-NBC-WSJ-poll.pdf.

7.   Nicolas Loris, "The Costs of Cap and Trade and The Costs of Doing Nothing," *The Foundry* (blog), October 15, 2009, http://blog.heritage.org/2009/10/15/the-costs-of-cap-and-trade-and-the-costs-of-doing-nothing.

8.   "Barney Frank in 2005: What Housing Bubble?" YouTube video, courtesy of www.verumserum.com June 27, 2005, http://www.youtube.com/watch?v=iW5qKYfqALE.

## CHAPTER 12. RUNNING FOR THE SENATE: 2011

1.   Chris Cillizza and Aaron Blake, "Can McCaskill weather her plane problem?" *The Washington Post,* March 22, 2011, http://www.washingtonpost.com/blogs/the-fix/post/can-claire-mccaskill-weather-her-plane-problem/2011/03/21/ABejuuBB_blog.html.

2.   Albert Samaha, "John Brunner Officially Enters U.S. Senate Race," *Daily RFT* (blog), October 4, 2011, http://blogs.riverfronttimes.com/dailyrft/2011/10/john_brunner_announces_senate.php.

3.   "St. Charles Manufacturer Runs for Senate," CBS St. Louis KMOX, October 3, 2011, http://stlouis.cbslocal.com/2011/10/03/st-charles-manufacturer-runs-for-u-s-senate.

4.   "Club for Growth PAC Disappointed By Akin Ad Defending Earmarks," Club for Growth, July 31, 2012, http://www.clubforgrowth.org/news/?id=1131&v=pr.

## CHAPTER 14. THE DANGEROUS CAMPAIGN TRAIL

1.   "Roy Blunt Pledges To Never Vote Like Roy Blunt Again," *Fired Up! Missouri*, http://firedupmissouri.com/node/12712.

## CHAPTER 15. REPUBLICAN PRIMARY HOME STRETCH: 2012

1.   Jo Mannies, "Is McCaskill choosing sides in the GOP primary? She says no, others aren't so sure," *St. Louis Beacon*, July 20, 2012, https://www.stlbeacon.org/#!/content/26170/mccaskill_attack_gop_072012.

2.   David Catanese, "With Todd Akin ad, Claire McCaskill meddles in GOP primary," *Politico*, July 19, 2012 (ad linked), http://www.politico.com/news/stories/0712/78737.html.

3.   Emily Schultheis, "McCaskill ad calls Akin 'too conservative' for Missouri," *Politico*, August 3, 2012, http://www.politico.com/blogs/burns-haberman/2012/08/mccaskill-ad-calls-akin-too-conservative-for-missouri-131032.html.

4.   Paige Winfield Cunningham, "McCaskill labels Todd Akin 'most conservative' in GOP primary," *Washington Times*, July 20, 2012, http://www.washingtontimes.com/blog/inside-politics/2012/jul/20/mccaskill-todd-akin-most-conservative-gop-primary.

5.   Brian Naylor, "GOP Has Big Hopes For Missouri Senate Race," NHPR, http://nhpr.org/post/gop-has-big-hopes-missouri-senate-race.

6.   Chris Good, "Sarah Palin Cuts TV Ad for Sarah Steelman in Missouri Senate Race," ABC News, July 30, 2012, http://abcnews.go.com/blogs/politics/2012/07/sarah-palin-cuts-tv-ad-for-sarah-steelman-in-missouri-senate-race.

7.   William Bradford, *Of Plymouth Plantation* (New York: McGraw Hill, 1981).

8.   Sermons, Truth in Action Ministries. http://www.djameskennedy.com/sermons/page:1.

9.   "2012 Missouri Senate Race: Todd Akin Victory Speech After Primary Election," YouTube video, posted by "Mike Wx," August 10, 2012, http://www.youtube.com/watch?v=E76GBOVwHis.

## CHAPTER 16. DAMAGE CONTROL

1.   "Hannity Urges Akin To Consider Dropping Out In Interview With Him," Real Clear Politics Video, August 20, 2012, http://www.realclearpolitics.com/video/2012/08/20/hannity_urges_akin_to_consider_dropping_out_in_interview_with_him.html.

2.   "Akin tells Huckabee he's staying in race," *CNN Politics* (blog), August 21, 2012, http://politicalticker.blogs.cnn.com/2012/08/21/akin-tells-huckabee-hes-staying-in-race/comment-page-1.

3.   Margaret Hartmann, "Authorities Investigate Rape and Death Threats Against Todd Akin," *New York*, August 23, 2012, http://nymag.com/daily/intelligencer/2012/08/todd-akin-receives-rape-death-threats.html.

4.  "Rep. Todd Akin Explains Comments about 'Legitimate Rape' on *Good Morning America*," YouTube video, posted by "PublicApologyCentral," August 22, 2102, https://www.youtube.com/watch?v=3KUtTiymOYY.


## CHAPTER 17. PLAYING HARDBALL

1.  Tim Craig and Michael Shear, "Allen Quip Provokes Outrage, Apology," *The Washington Post*, August 15, 2006, http://www.washingtonpost.com/wp-dyn/content/article/2006/08/14/AR2006081400589.html.

2.  Yuval Levin, "Obama and the Born-Alive Act," *The Corner* (blog), National Review Online, August 11, 2008, http://www.nationalreview.com/corner/166906/obama-and-born-alive-act/yuval-levin.

3.  "'Jane Roe' Tells True Story Behind Roe v. Wade: Norma McCorvey Says 'Pure and simple. I lied,'" The Free Library, http://www.thefreelibrary.com/%22Jane+Roe%22+Tells+True+Story+Behind+Roe+v.+Wade+Norma+McCorvey+Says...-a055342471.

4.  "Full Transcript of *NBC Dateline* report on Juanita Broaddrick," posted on shadowgov.com, http://www.shadowgov.com/Clinton/DNBCJuanitaTranscript.html.

5.  Candice E. Jackson, *Their Lives: The Women Targeted by the Clinton Machine* (Los Angeles: World Ahead Publishing, 2005), 42.

6.  Patrick Goldstein, "Judge 'The Pianist,' not Roman Polanski," March 4, 2003, *Los Angeles Times*, http://articles.latimes.com/2003/mar/04/entertainment/et-gold4.

7.  Maev Kennedy, "Polanski was not guilty of 'rape-rape', says Whoopi Goldberg," *The Guardian*, September 29, 2009, http://www.theguardian.com/film/2009/sep/29/roman-polanski-whoopi-goldberg.

8.  Michael O'Brien, "Romney: Akin's rape comments 'insulting, inexcusable,'" NBC News, August 20, 2012, http://firstread.nbcnews.com/_news/2012/08/20/13376147-romney-akins-rape-comments-insulting-inexcusable?lite.

9.  Chris Gentilviso, "Todd Akin On Abortion: 'Legitimate Rape' Victims Have 'Ways To Try To Shut That Whole Thing Down,'" *Huffington Post*, August 19, 2012, http://www.huffingtonpost.com/2012/08/19/todd-akin-abortion-legitimate-rape_n_1807381.html.

10.  Jaco, "Jaco Report: Full Interview With Todd Akin," (see chap. 2, n. 1).

11.  "Cornyn: Akin 'Should Carefully Consider What Is Best For Him' And The GOP," *TPM Livewire* (blog), August 20, 2012, http://talkingpointsmemo.com/livewire/cornyn-akin-should-carefully-consider-what-is-best-for-him-and-the-gop.


## CHAPTER 18. PILING ON

1.  Melissa Jeltsen, "Todd Akin Goes After Reince Priebus: He Has A 'Personal Vendetta,'" *Huffington Post*, August 28, 2012, http://www.huffingtonpost.com/2012/08/28/todd-akin-goes-after-rein_n_1837168.html.

2.   Caleb Howe, "Priebus on Akin: 'He Could Be Tied, We're Not Going To Send Him A Penny,'" *RedState* (blog), August 27, 2012, http://www.redstate.com/2012/08/27/priebus-on-akin-he-could-be-tied-were-not-going-to-send-him-a-penny.

3.   Sheelah Kolhatkar, "Exclusive: Inside Karl Rove's Billionaire Fundraiser," *Bloomberg Business-Week* (blog), http://www.businessweek.com/articles/2012-08-31/exclusive-inside-karl-roves-billionaire-fundraiser.

4.   Meenal Vamburkar, "Karl Rove: If Akin's 'Found Mysteriously Murdered, Don't Look For My Whereabouts!'" *Mediaite* (blog), August 31, 2012, http://www.mediaite.com/online/karl-rove-if-akins-found-mysteriously-murdered-dont-look-for-my-whereabouts.

5.   Tim Mak, "Report: Karl Rove make [*sic*] Todd Akin murder joke," *Politico*, August 31, 2012, http://politi.co/1dB9N2u.

6.   Andy Barr, "Karl Rove: Christine O'Donnell said 'nutty things,'" *Politico*, September 15, 2010, http://www.politico.com/news/stories/0910/42205.html.

## CHAPTER 19. FIRING BACK

1.   Elicia Dover, "Newt Gingrich Fundraising For Embattled Todd Akin," ABC News, September 19, 2012, http://abcnews.go.com/blogs/politics/2012/09/newt-gingrich-fundraising-for-todd-akin-monday.

2.   Brian Naylor, "Akin Faces Another Deadline To Leave Senate Race," September 25, 2012, npr.org, http://www.npr.org/2012/09/25/161726862/akin-faces-another-deadline-to-leave-senate-race.

3.   Eric Metaxas, "Ending Gendercide: 200 Million Missing Girls in China, India," *LifeNews.com* (blog), November 19, 2012, http://www.lifenews.com/2012/11/19/ending-gendercide-200-million-missing-girls-in-china-india.

4.   Naylor, "Akin Faces Another Deadline," (see n. 2).

5.   "Phyllis Schlafly Calls on Karl Rove to Resign," *Eagle Forum* (blog), September 1, 2012, http://blog.eagleforum.org/2012/09/phyllis-schlafly-calls-on-karl-rove-to.html?m=1.

6.   Ibid.

7.   "Ann Coulter Introduces Phyllis Schlafly at David Horowitz's Restoration Weekend," YouTube video, posted by "BrianGreco TV," November 25, 2012, http://www.youtube.com/watch?v=pOaK88u2oc4.

8.   Ryan Bomberger, "As Someone Born After Rape, I Say Todd Akin Shouldn't Step Aside," *The Bunker* (blog), August 22, 2012, http://www.lifenews.com/2012/08/22/as-someone-born-after-rape-i-say-todd-akin-shouldnt-step-aside.

9.   Dean Murphy, "Mrs. Clinton Portrays Lazio as Bully and Derides His Tax Plan," *The New York Times*, September 19, 2000, http://www.nytimes.com/2000/09/19/nyregion/mrs-clinton-portrays-lazio-as-bully-and-derides-his-tax-plan.html.

10. "That Time Rick Lazio Invaded Hillary's Space," *Althouse* (blog), November 25, 2007, http://althouse.blogspot.com/2007/11/that-time-rick-lazio-invaded-hillarys.html.

11. "Missouri Senate Debate: Sen Claire McCaskill, Congressman Todd Akin & Libertarian Jonathan Dine," YouTube video, posted by "MOXNEWSd0tC0M," September 24, 2012, http://www.youtube.com/watch?v=BEp75ILbqA8.

12. Yael Abouhalkah, "McCaskill destroys Akin in debate," *The Kansas City Star,* September 24, 2012, http://voices.kansascity.com/entries/mccaskill-destroys-akin-debate.

13. Rachel Weiner, "Todd Akin: Claire McCaskill was more 'ladylike' in 2006," *The Washington Post,* September 27, 2012, http://www.washingtonpost.com/blogs/post-politics/wp/2012/09/27/akin-mccaskill-was-more-ladylike-in-2006.

14. John McCormack, "Ann Coulter to Todd Akin: If You're Really Pro-Life, You'll Drop Out of the Senate Race," *The Weekly Standard,* August 20, 2012, https://www.weeklystandard.com/blogs/ann-coulter-todd-akin-if-youre-really-pro-life-youll-drop-out-senate-race_650298.html.

15. Winston Churchill, "Never Give In," The Churchill Centre, October 29, 1941, https://www.winstonchurchill.org/learn/speeches/speeches-of-winston-churchill/103-never-give-in.

## CHAPTER 20. BACKFIRE

1. Eric Kleefeld, "GOP Senate Candidates Lining Up Against Todd Akin," *A Shred of Truth* (blog), August 20, 2012, http://shredoftruth.com/home/gop-senate-candidates-lining-up-against-todd-akin.html.

2. Paul Blumenthal, "Senate Races 2012: Republican Establishment Tries To Tamp Down Tea Party Insurgency," *Huffington Post,* April 19, 2012, http://www.huffingtonpost.com/2012/04/19/senate-races-2012-republican-establishment-tea-party_n_1437646.html.

3. Susan Milligan, "Richard Mourdock's Todd Akin Moment," *USNews* (blog), October 24, 2012, http://www.usnews.com/opinion/blogs/susan-milligan/2012/10/24/richard-mour-docks-todd-akin-moment.

4. Brian Francisco, "Mourdock denounced, defended," journalgazette.net, October 24, 2012, http://www.journalgazette.net/article/20121024/LOCAL08/121029767/1002/LOCAL.

5. William Saletan, "The Party of Rape," *Slate,* January 14, 2013, http://www.slate.com/articles/health_and_science/human_nature/2013/01/phil_gingrey_todd_akin_and_richard_mourdock_the_gop_s_rape_problem_is_spreading.html.

6. Milligan, "Richard Mourdock's Todd Akin Moment" (see n. 3).

7. Elise Viebeck, "Abortion-rights groups cheer Akin, Mourdock defeats," *The Hill,* November 7, 2012, http://thehill.com/blogs/healthwatch/politics-elections/266507-abortion-rights-groups-cheer-akin-mourdock-defeats.

8. Katrina Trinko, "Mourdock Isn't Second Akin," *The Corner* (blog), National Review Online, October 23, 2012, http://www.nationalreview.com/corner/331460/mourdock-isnt-second-akin-katrina-trinko.

9. Richard Murdoch said in an October 2012 press release and was reported on by Gregory J. Krieg and Chris Good, "Murdock Rape Comment Puts GOP on Defense," ABC News, October 24, 2012, http://abcnews.go.com/Politics/OTUS/richard-mourdock-rape-comment-puts-romney-defense/story?id=17552263.

10. Fred Barnes, "The Great Divide," *The Weekly Standard*, November 18, 2013, http://www.weeklystandard.com/articles/great-divide_766431.html.

11. Ibid.

12. Gallup, Abortion Poll, May 2–7, 2013, http://www.gallup.com/poll/1576/abortion.aspx#1.

13. Barnes, "The Great Divide," (see n. 10).

14. William Kristol, "Debbie Wasserman Akin," *The Weekly Standard,* September 5, 2012, http://www.weeklystandard.com/blogs/debbie-wasserman-akin_651711.html.

15. James Hohmann, "Reince Priebus calls on GOP to improve 'tone,'" *Politico,* January 24, 2014, http://www.politico.com/story/2014/01/reince-priebus-gop-tone-102566.html.

16. As quoted in Patrick Buchanan, "A Grand Old Party in Panic," cnsnews.com, August 24, 2012, http://cnsnews.com/blog/patrick-j-buchanan/grand-old-party-panic.

17. Peter Marshall and David Manuel, *The Light and the Glory: 1492–1793* (Grand Rapids, MI: Revell, 2009), 390.

18. Abraham Lincoln, "Last Public Address," April 11, 1865, Abraham Lincoln Online, http://www.abrahamlincolnonline.org/lincoln/speeches/last.htm.

19. Ronald Reagan, "Farewell Address to the Nation," January 11, 1989, American Rhetoric, http://www.americanrhetoric.com/speeches/ronaldreaganfarewelladdress.html.

## CHAPTER 21. REVIVAL

1. Lucia Graves, "Todd Akin: 'At The Heart Of Liberalism Is Really A Hatred Of God,'" *Huffington Post*, June 27, 2011, http://www.huffingtonpost.com/2011/06/27/todd-akin-at-the-heart-of-liberalism-hatred-of-god_n_885280.html.

2. Ben Shapiro, "Resurrection: DNC Overrules Delegates, Rams God and Jerusalem Back into Platform," Breitbart, September 5, 2012, http://www.breitbart.com/Big-Government/2012/09/05/Democrats-change-platform-God-Israel.

## CHAPTER 22. SCORCHED EARTH

1. "U.S. arms production during WW2 from 1939–1945," WW2 Weapons, http://ww2-weapons.com/History/Production/Anglo-Americans/US.htm.

2. Dan Holler, "Congress to Constituents: It's Your Fault," Townhall.com, September 17, 2012, http://townhall.com/columnists/danholler/2012/09/17/congress_to_constituents_its_your_fault/page/full.

3. David Sherfinski, "Sen. Claire McCaskill on Obamacare: 'The store is open and we've locked the front door,'" *The Washington Times,* November 14, 2013, http://www.washingtontimes.com/news/2013/nov/14/sen-claire-mccaskill-obamacare-store-open-and-weve.

4. Jo Mannies, "McCaskill highlights differences with Akin over Social Security, Medicare," St. Louis Beacon, August 19, 2102, https://www.stlbeacon.org/#!/content/27123/mccaskill_medicare_091912.

5. "Unfit," YouTube video, posted by ClaireMcCaskill2012's channel, November 1, 2012, https://www.youtube.com/watch?v=wnlftrToH1g.

6. "McCaskill up narrowly, Romney and Nixon by wider margins," Public Policy Polling, November 4, 2012, http://www.publicpolicypolling.com/main/2012/11/mccaskill-up-narrowly-romney-and-nixon-by-wider-margins.html.

7. Jo Mannies, "Missouri's U.S. Senate contest gets last-minute jolt from old anti-abortion arrests and Larry Flynt," *St. Louis Beacon,* November 4, 2012, https://www.stlbeacon.org/#!/content/27870/mosen_arrests_flynt_110412.

8. "Todd Akin references God in concession speech," *USA Today* video, November 6, 2012, http://www.usatoday.com/videos/news/politics/2012/11/06/1688105.

9. "God Makes No Mistakes: Todd Akin's Outrageous Concession Speech," WorldNEWS, November 6, 2012, http://appv1.linktv.org/videos/todd-akin-bites-the-dust.

10. Charlie Cook, "Senate Democrats Earned Every Seat They Won, Thanks to the DSCC," *National Journal,* November 15, 2012, http://www.nationaljournal.com/columns/cook-report/senate-democrats-earned-every-seat-they-won-thanks-to-the-dscc-20121115.

## CONCLUSION: A TIME FOR HEROES

1. Although widely attributed to Tocqueville, there is no definitive source.

# INDEX

Thank you for choosing to read

# FIRING BACK

If you enjoyed this book, we hope that you will tell your friends
and family. There are many ways to spread the word:

Share your thoughts on Facebook, your blog,
or Tweet "You should read #FIRING BACK by Todd Akin // @worldnetdaily"

Consider recommending the book to your book club.

LIKE the book on Facebook at www.facebook.com/WNDNews.

Send a copy to someone you know who would benefit from reading this book.

Write a review online at Amazon.com or BN.com
Subscribe to WND at www.wnd.com
Visit the WND Superstore at superstore.wnd.com

WND BOOKS

A WND COMPANY • WASHINGTON DC • WNDBOOKS.COM

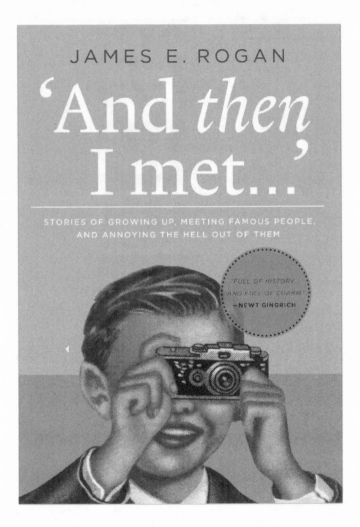

# WND Books

PRESENTS

Bigger than Watergate! Bigger than Iran-Contra! Ten times bigger than both, said one representative. The Benghazi scandal may have been covered up by the White House, but the truth is about to come out. *The Real Benghazi Story* is a ground-breaking investigative work that finally exposes some of the most significant issues related to the murderous September 11, 2012, attack-information with current national security implications.

**WND BOOKS** • A **WND** COMPANY • WASHINGTON DC • WNDBOOKS.COM

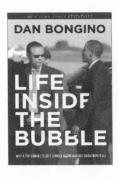
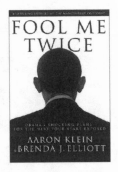

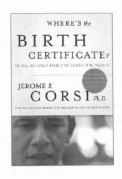

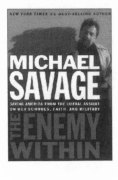
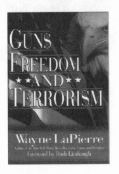
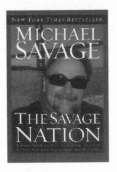